OPPOSING VIEWPOINTS® SERIES

Population

Other Books of Related Interest:

Opposing Viewpoints Series

Cloning

Poverty

The US Census

At Issue Series

Food Insecurity

Pandemics

Should Parents Be Allowed to Choose the Gender of Their Children?

Current Controversies Series

Developing Nations

Illegal Immigration

Pollution

"Congress shall make
no law . . . abridging
the freedom of speech,
or of the press."

First Amendment to the US Constitution

The basic foundation of our democracy is the First Amendment guarantee of freedom of expression. The Opposing Viewpoints Series is dedicated to the concept of this basic freedom and the idea that it is more important to practice it than to enshrine it.

OPPOSING
VIEWPOINTS®
SERIES

Population

David Haugen and Susan Musser, Book Editors

GREENHAVEN PRESS
A part of Gale, Cengage Learning

GALE
CENGAGE Learning·

Detroit • New York • San Francisco • New Haven, Conn • Waterville, Maine • London

Elizabeth Des Chenes, *Managing Editor*

© 2012 Greenhaven Press, a part of Gale, Cengage Learning.

Gale and Greenhaven Press are registered trademarks used herein under license.

For more information, contact:
Greenhaven Press
27500 Drake Rd.
Farmington Hills, MI 48331-3535
Or you can visit our Internet site at gale.cengage.com

Articles in Greenhaven Press anthologies are often edited for length to meet page require-ments. In addition, original titles of these works are changed to clearly present the main thesis and to explicitly indicate the author's opinion. Every effort is made to ensure that Greenhaven Press accurately reflects the original intent of the authors. Every effort has been made to trace the owners of copyrighted material.

Cover image copyright © Rudy Sulgan/Encyclopedia/Corbis.

LIBRARY OF CONGRESS CATALOGING-IN-PUBLICATION DATA

Population / David Haugen and Susan Musser, book editors.
    p. cm. -- (Opposing viewpoints)
    Includes bibliographical references and index.
    ISBN 978-0-7377-5755-2 (hardcover : alk. paper) -- ISBN 978-0-7377-5756-9 (pbk. : alk. paper)
    1. Population 2. Population--Environmental aspects 3. Population--Economic as-pects I. Haugen, David M., 1969- II. Musser, Susan
    HB871.P62953 2011
    363.9--dc23

                                           2011023561

Printed in the United States of America
1 2 3 4 5 6 7 15 14 13 12 11

Contents

Chapter 3: How Should Population Growth Be Addressed?

Chapter 4: What Will Be the Impact of Global Demographic Shifts?

Why Consider Opposing Viewpoints?

> "The only way in which a human being can make some approach to knowing the whole of a subject is by hearing what can be said about it by persons of every variety of opinion and studying all modes in which it can be looked at by every character of mind. No wise man ever acquired his wisdom in any mode but this."
>
> *John Stuart Mill*

In our media-intensive culture it is not difficult to find differing opinions. Thousands of newspapers and magazines and dozens of radio and television talk shows resound with differing points of view. The difficulty lies in deciding which opinion to agree with and which "experts" seem the most credible. The more inundated we become with differing opinions and claims, the more essential it is to hone critical reading and thinking skills to evaluate these ideas. Opposing Viewpoints books address this problem directly by presenting stimulating debates that can be used to enhance and teach these skills. The varied opinions contained in each book examine many different aspects of a single issue. While examining these conveniently edited opposing views, readers can develop critical thinking skills such as the ability to compare and contrast authors' credibility, facts, argumentation styles, use of persuasive techniques, and other stylistic tools. In short, the Opposing Viewpoints Series is an ideal way to attain the higher-level thinking and reading skills so essential in a culture of diverse and contradictory opinions.

In addition to providing a tool for critical thinking, Opposing Viewpoints books challenge readers to question their own strongly held opinions and assumptions. Most people form their opinions on the basis of upbringing, peer pressure, and personal, cultural, or professional bias. By reading carefully balanced opposing views, readers must directly confront new ideas as well as the opinions of those with whom they disagree. This is not to argue simplistically that everyone who reads opposing views will—or should—change his or her opinion. Instead, the series enhances readers' understanding of their own views by encouraging confrontation with opposing ideas. Careful examination of others' views can lead to the readers' understanding of the logical inconsistencies in their own opinions, perspective on why they hold an opinion, and the consideration of the possibility that their opinion requires further evaluation.

Evaluating Other Opinions

To ensure that this type of examination occurs, Opposing Viewpoints books present all types of opinions. Prominent spokespeople on different sides of each issue as well as well-known professionals from many disciplines challenge the reader. An additional goal of the series is to provide a forum for other, less known, or even unpopular viewpoints. The opinion of an ordinary person who has had to make the decision to cut off life support from a terminally ill relative, for example, may be just as valuable and provide just as much insight as a medical ethicist's professional opinion. The editors have two additional purposes in including these less known views. One, the editors encourage readers to respect others' opinions—even when not enhanced by professional credibility. It is only by reading or listening to and objectively evaluating others' ideas that one can determine whether they are worthy of consideration. Two, the inclusion of such viewpoints encourages the important critical thinking skill of objectively evaluating an author's credentials and bias. This evaluation will illuminate an author's reasons for taking a particular stance on an issue and will aid in readers' evaluation of the author's ideas.

It is our hope that these books will give readers a deeper understanding of the issues debated and an appreciation of the complexity of even seemingly simple issues when good and honest people disagree. This awareness is particularly important in a democratic society such as ours in which people enter into public debate to determine the common good. Those with whom one disagrees should not be regarded as enemies but rather as people whose views deserve careful examination and may shed light on one's own.

Thomas Jefferson once said that "difference of opinion leads to inquiry, and inquiry to truth." Jefferson, a broadly educated man, argued that "if a nation expects to be ignorant and free . . . it expects what never was and never will be." As individuals and as a nation, it is imperative that we consider the opinions of others and examine them with skill and discernment. The Opposing Viewpoints Series is intended to help readers achieve this goal.

David L. Bender and Bruno Leone,
Founders

Introduction

> *"The increase of the human species can only be kept commensurate to the increase of the means of subsistence by the constant operation of the strong law of necessity acting as a check upon the greater power. . . . The effects of this check on man [is] complicated. Impelled to the increase of his species by [a] powerful instinct, reason interrupts his career and asks him whether he may not bring beings into the world for whom he cannot provide the means of subsistence."*
>
> —Thomas Malthus,
> eighteenth-century British scholar
> of political economy

In April 2011, the global human population exceeded 6.9 billion individuals. Since 2006, the world has added 400 million people, and by 2016, the US Census predicts another 380 million will fill the planet. Of those expected newcomers, the Population Reference Bureau (PRB) maintains that 97 percent will be born in Asia, Africa, Latin America, and the Caribbean. Asia is the home to the largest human population (over 3.8 billion people), and though birth rates have declined in many Asian and Pacific countries, the continent is expected to remain the home of around 60 percent of the earth's population for many decades. Africa's population growth rate is also quite high. While it currently has fewer than 1 billion people, the fertility rate in several Sub-Saharan African countries exceeds five births per woman, according to the World Bank. Writing for that institution, Wolfgang Fengler, a leading economist in Africa, asserts that "by 2050, Africa will be home to more than 20 percent of the world's population." Fengler maintains that the rapid growth of Africa has been abetted not merely by more births but by longer life spans afforded by better health care.

In an October 2005 article for the *African Executive*, James Kathuri, a lecturer at Kenyatta University in Kenya, argues that Africa's population growth was "a blessing." In his view, other high-population countries like India and China have experienced economic growth precisely because of their large labor pools. He hopes African governments would see their growing numbers of young people as a means to revamp farming and industrial practices to take advantage of human capital. Kathuri insists that "high populations can and should be supported to steer nations particularly in Africa into agriculture and industrial revolutions." Indeed, the opportunities for countries with "youth bulges" are often set against the problems of nations that are experiencing declining fertility rates and aging populations. Most developed economies, for example, are witnessing birthrates below replacement levels; consequently, there are too few working-age individuals to take care of the rising number of older people and provide the finances to fill pensions and welfare plans. According to the *World Population Highlights: Key Findings from the PRB's 2010 World Population Data Sheet*, "The number of retiring workers [in developed countries] each year will eventually exceed the number of new workers into the labor market. . . . The ratio of older nonworking people per worker will almost double by 2050, putting a strain on government social support and public finances." Thus some observers argue that having a higher birthrate can ensure that there will be enough working-age individuals to drive economies and tend to the needs of the expanding older demographic.

Though some, like Kathuri, might see the prospect of more workers as a benefit to economic development, others heed the warnings of Thomas Malthus, a British political economist whose work in the late eighteenth and early nineteenth centuries focused on the potential problems of overpopulation. Malthus looked back over past historical eras and noted that when populations increased, social ills such as wars, disease, and oppression of the lower classes ensued. He maintained the cause of these social ills was often too many people fighting for too few resources. Today, Malthus's scholarly heirs advance arguments along the same lines. Some warn that countries experiencing "youth bulges" often suffer increased civil unrest and violence as young people act out against the lack of jobs, repression, or traditional images of authority. Such unruliness, however, is typically subsumed by broader arguments about the presumed shortages of natural resources that will foster more dissent between the haves and the have-nots. Cornell University professors David and Marcia Pimentel wrote an article for *World Futures* in 2003 that asserted, "If all people in the world could enjoy a standard of living and energy consumption rate similar to that of the average American and the world population continued to grow at a rate of 1.5%, the world's fossil fuel reserves are estimated to last only about 15 years." Even at current, unequal rates of consumption, many researchers have estimated that oil stocks may be depleted by 2040.

Beyond oil, the Pimentels and others tie growing populations to strains on arable cropland and freshwater resources. In a Winter 2009 *World Policy Journal* interview, Ismail Serageldin, former World Bank vice president for environmentally and socially sustainable development, claimed, "In general, over the past century, there has been a three-fold increase in population, but a six-fold increase in water consumption. So, though population is increasing, the amount of water consumed per person is accelerating. As a result, demand for water is very high." Serageldin already attributes some conflict— such as the civil war in Darfur, Sudan, that began in 2003—as arising from drought and water shortages; he warns that, unless the world adopts better water management, regions such as the Middle East could easily erupt in violence over water security.

Whether such dire predictions will come to pass is still a subject of great debate. In a world that witnesses over 360,000 births and 154,000 deaths each day (according to the US Census), the difference may be interpreted as a contributing factor to such impending resource catastrophes or a resource itself that may help the planet sustain humanity's growth. In *Opposing Viewpoints: Population*, these types of arguments are presented for consideration in chapters that ask What Concerns Surround Population Growth? What Problems Might Be Attributed to Population Growth? How Should Population Growth Be Addressed? and What Will Be the Impact of Global Demographic Shifts? The various experts that debate the issues herein may alternatively trumpet or dismiss the burden of population growth, but all recognize that the planet's human population is growing and that governments, economies, and other social structures will need—indeed, be compelled—to adapt to such changes to sustain current populations and the 360,000 newcomers who arrive each day.

CHAPTER 1

What Concerns Surround Population Growth?

Chapter Preface

In 1968, fears of catastrophic global harm resulting from runaway population growth reached a pinnacle with the publication of the book *The Population Bomb* by Paul R. Ehrlich. In this book, written with his wife, Anne, Ehrlich warned of the imminent consequences of overpopulation, such as food shortages, social unrest, and environmental degradation. In the more than forty years since the publication of this seminal work, the Ehrlichs have remained outspoken about the dangers of overpopulation. Writing in the magazine *New Scientist* in 2006, the pair defended their argument that the optimal population of the planet was 2 billion people, which was the global population in 1930 and is less than one-third of the world's current population. In this same magazine in 2009, they echoed earlier grim predictions of resource strain and environmental decline and renewed their calls for increased focus on this issue stating, "Humanity needs to get behind a global discussion on these issues. . . . A major element of that discussion must be how to end the growth of the total human population humanely. . . . If that can be done, then a sustainable future for civilization might be possible."

In the wake of prophecies from the Ehrlichs and others like them, overpopulation has come to be widely viewed as an apocalyptic crisis. Still, many researchers and commentators decry these dire forecasts as alarmist at best and, in many cases, the pretext for the development of harmful, discriminatory population control programs. One of the most outspoken critics of an overpopulation crisis is Steven W. Mosher, the president of the Population Research Institute (PRI), an organization that seeks to "expose the myth of overpopulation, to expose human rights abuses committed in population control programs, and to make the case that people are the world's greatest resource." Writing on the PRI blog in February 2011,

Mosher announced his excitement about the pending arrival of the seven billionth human on planet earth. This baby, he claims, will be "born into a world that is more prosperous than our forebears could have imagined." Mosher emphasizes the increases in per-capita income, longevity, and resource production coupled with declines in infant mortality, all in the face of an ever-growing human population, as evidence that the world is on a path of improvement and humanity is flourishing, not languishing in a state of imminent catastrophe.

As arguments like those of the Ehrlichs and Mosher dominate the conversation about overpopulation, there has been little in the way of a consensus reached as to whether an ongoing population increase will harm or benefit the planet and humanity. While the population continues to grow as a whole and the question of overpopulation's impact remains, fertility declines in regions such as Europe and Japan have raised new questions about whether all population growth is equal in its effect and if discussion about this growth yields real solutions or just a perverse discrimination. The authors in the following chapter debate issues of concern relating to population growth.

> *"One of the most serious challenges to human destiny ... will be the growth of population."*

Global Population Growth Poses a Serious Challenge

Michael Fritz

Recent estimates from the United Nations predict that the world's population will continue to increase until the year 2050 before reaching its peak at around 9.2 billion people. Many scientists, economists, and commentators have argued that this growth will have a devastating impact on the planet and human life if something is not done to defuse the population bomb. In the viewpoint that follows, Michael Fritz takes this stance, arguing that the somewhat conservative increase proposed by the UN will make it impossible to address issues like global warming, energy independence, and regional conflict. These issues are all closely tied to population growth, contends the author, and it is necessary that the United States and the rest of the Western world take proactive steps to limit the continual increase in population and save the planet from destruction. Michael Fritz is a senior foreign service officer who works for the United States Agency for International Development.

Michael Fritz, "Speaking Out: The Population Bomb Is Still Ticking," *Foreign Service Journal*, vol. 87, January 2010. Copyright © 2010 by Foreign Service Journal. All rights reserved. Reproduced by permission.

As you read, consider the following questions:

1. By how many people does the UN predict the population will increase by the year 2050, according to the author?

2. According to Fritz, how would half the world's switching to hybrid cars impact problems such as global warming, urban growth, and congestion?

3. What is "the most important step in creating sustainable communities," as stated by the author?

[A merican biologist] Paul Ehrlich's 1968 book, *The Population Bomb*, hit America's college campuses with the intellectual force of a futurist's improvised explosive device. It challenged Americans to consider—many for the first time—the potential for chaos and upheaval hidden within unfolding global demographic trends.

A student at the time, I still vividly recall the power of Ehrlich's message: the explosive growth of the human race affects all issues on the global agenda, from regional conflict and habitat loss to depletion of energy, food and water resources.

That premise is truer today than ever before. In fact, it obligates us to take action. Unless population size is factored into policy decisions, we will never achieve valid, sustainable solutions to problems like global warming and energy independence. So if we care about the future of our children, then we need to be concerned about the effects of population growth on each and every one of those issues.

The Staggering Growth to Come

There are all sorts of population growth scenarios, but a frequently cited one comes from the United Nations Population Division. It forecasts that by 2050, the number of humans on the planet will have grown by a third, from 6.7 billion to 9.2

billion, before leveling off. That increase—2.5 billion human beings—is equal to the entire global population in 1950.

Paradoxically, it will be the poorest, least developed nations that see the greatest growth in population, as their population rises from 5.4 billion to 7.9 billion. Staggering as such numbers are, they are actually quite conservative, for they assume a rise in contraceptive use, coupled with a decline in fertility. (The calculations also factor in deaths from HIV/AIDS, as well as projected migration patterns.)

Specifically, the figure assumes that fertility will continue to decline in developing countries, from 2.75 children per woman to 2.05 children per woman by 2050. (The degree of fertility reduction projected for the 50 least developed countries is even sharper: from 4.63 children per woman in 2005–2010 to 2.50 children per woman in 2045–2050.)

Given the fact that even the tiniest variation in fertility rates can have huge implications for the size of the eventual world population, and taking into account the lack of family planning access in much of the world, 9.2 billion may well be a "best case" scenario.

The Role of the United States

Historically, the U.S. conducted a strong population assistance program that enjoyed consistent bipartisan support through numerous administrations. Its longstanding policy objectives have been to enhance the freedom of individuals to choose the number and spacing of their children, and to encourage population growth consistent with the growth of economic resources and productivity.

There is also a strong rationale for population assistance in terms of improving maternal and child health. Various justifications for this have held sway at different times, but all are important. Many factors lead to people having fewer children: female education, improved child survival, access to contraception, and economic growth that offers opportunities to women outside the home, changing the calculus for how they most productively spend their time.

Of all of these, access to contraception is one of the easiest to implement, has the most direct effect, and has had measurable success. Average family size has fallen by half in the developing world since the 1960s, and contraceptive use has increased from under 10 percent to over 50 percent.

Yet while all these programs affect population growth, none has population reduction as an explicit goal. In fact, over the past decade serious discussion of these issues has been conspicuously lacking in the United States, in both the foreign and domestic policy debates.

[Former vice president] Al Gore's 2006 movie, *An Inconvenient Truth*, gave much of the world a wake-up call on global warming. In my opinion, however, he missed an opportunity to link these problems to population growth.

Take a simple example. Even if half the world switched to hybrid cars, that would help only marginally with global warming, urban growth and congestion, habitat loss, and other key problems. This is because rapidly growing populations in the developing world are demanding more and more automobiles. (China and India are already mass-producing large numbers of vehicles for their own needs.)

Yes, perhaps the economic crisis has slowed that process down. But let's not believe that the trend won't resume once economic conditions are more favorable—unless we promote a different perspective. In fact, the global economic slowdown presents us with a unique opportunity, a golden moment in which we must rethink the meaning of community and the means to achieve this new vision.

Fortunately, Washington's status as the largest bilateral donor in the field of population assistance gives us a platform to exert global leadership in framing the issue. The [Barack] Obama administration's Fiscal Year 2010 request for State and

USAID's [United States Agency for International Development] family planning and reproductive health programs totals $593 million.

The West Must Be a Role Model

As Ehrlich wrote four decades ago, addressing population growth is the key to the big-picture issues in the developing and developed world. We need to ask ourselves what kind of communities we want to live in—and then ask the same question of the citizens of other countries.

In an era of dwindling oil supplies and rising energy costs, the need for low-energy lifestyles has never been greater. In fact, energy efficiency is one of the top priorities for many of our host-country government counterparts. New Urbanism design principles and practices bring together the ideas and plans to create enjoyable places in which to live and work, while greatly reducing energy use.

Designing away the need for cars is the most important step in creating sustainable communities. This has the triple effect of lowering our energy use (especially imported energy), reducing global warming and raising our quality of life in cities by increasing mobility and convenience.

Yet for most on the cutting edge of New Urbanism, population, which should be an obvious factor, is not even mentioned. The world simply cannot afford for everyone to consume as we have in recent years, even though that is largely what the rest of the world aspires to do.

We in the West are bad role models. We must change our own behavior at the same time that we are asking others to change theirs. In a March [2010] *New York Times* column, [American journalist and author] Thomas Friedman suggested that we are all part of a gigantic Ponzi scheme [financial fraud] where we are living beyond our financial and economic means. Perhaps, Friedman opined, in our journey down the road of continuous growth we have hit the proverbial wall.

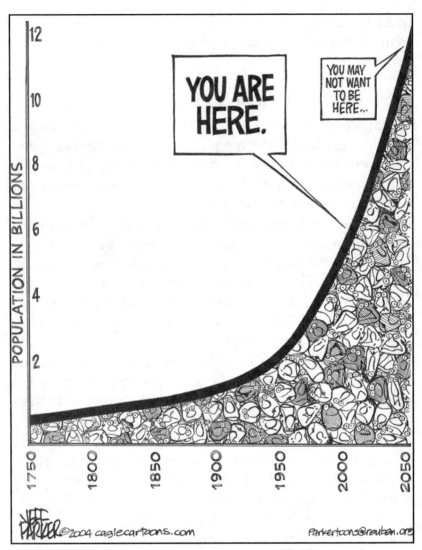

A Serious Challenge to Human Destiny

There are signs that the population bomb is beginning to attract serious attention again. In 2008, *Time* magazine published a commentary in which General Michael Hayden, a former director of the Central Intelligence Agency, warned that the sheer size of the projected increase in population could fuel instability and extremism, exacerbate climate change and make food and fuel even scarcer.

Similarly, the December 2009 edition of *Scientific American* includes a commentary by [American economist] Jeffrey D. Sachs titled "Can We Feed *and* Save the Planet?", in which he contends that the challenges of population control and food production need to be tackled in tandem.

And *Live Science* recently posted a story titled: "Save the Planet: Have Fewer Kids." Op-eds have also appeared in various publications arguing for more funding for family planning.

Given that population growth is the essential multiplier for any number of human ills, I call on my fellow professionals in development and diplomacy not just to monitor and report on the debate, but to lead the discussion.

A 1969 quote from [then US president] Richard Nixon reminds us that we've remained too silent for far too long: "One of the most serious challenges to human destiny in the last third of this century will be the growth of population. Whether man's response to that challenge will be a cause for pride or for despair in the year 2000 will depend very much on what we do today."

| "We are moving towards negative rates of growth, and stabilization at a lower population size."

The Facts Refute Alarmist Concerns over Global Population Growth

New Internationalist

While many politicians, scientists, and other experts have been calling attention to the impending doom that accompanies projected population growth, the New Internationalist *counters the concern that population growth is a runaway problem that will continue to increase and that threatens the world. To support this contradiction to alarmist claims, the author points out in the following viewpoint that fertility levels worldwide are decreasing and many countries are below replacement level, meaning that those populations are not even reproducing enough offspring to maintain their current size. As a result, the author insists that while there are some relevant concerns that accompany continued growth of the planet's population, particularly environmental ones, concerns about a population explosion are exaggerated. The* New Internationalist *is the magazine of the nonprofit cooperative of the same name that addresses contem-*

"The Population Panic," *New Internationalist*, January 2010, pp. 5–8. Copyright © 2010 by New Internationalist. All rights reserved. Reproduced by permission.

porary issues affecting the world, focusing mainly on the imbalance of power and wealth that, in its view, creates oppression worldwide.

As you read, consider the following questions:

1. As stated by the author, what is the global average number of children that each woman bears in her lifetime?

2. In how many countries has the fertility rate decreased to below replacement level, according to the *New Internationalist?*

3. What does the author identify as the connection between education and fertility rates?

Two small boys are picking olives off a tree in the central reservation on the road leading to the Palais de Congràes in downtown Marrakech, where the [2009] week-long international conference on population is about to begin. The boys place the olives in a bag before moving on to the next tree.

That's it! That's what's missing. Small boys!

I had been trying to work out why Morocco felt so different on this occasion compared with my two previous visits to the country. The first, in 1975, left me with a memory of being constantly besieged by gangs of small—and not so small—boys. They were offering their services as guides or porters or protectors from other boys offering their services as guides, porters or protectors. . . .

On my second visit, in 1987, I was doing a feature for the UN Population Fund which involved following the story of a woman who had just gone into labour. Back in her village a couple of days after the birth, the young mother still looked exhausted. She said she did not want any more children. Five was enough. 'She seems quite determined,' I commented to the midwife who had arranged the visit. She shrugged. 'Maybe. But her husband wants to have more. It's a question of status for him.'

Since then, Morocco has experienced a sharp decline in its fertility rate. Instead of women having seven or eight children, as they did in the 1960s and 1970s, they now have two or three.

Fertility Is Declining Worldwide

I flick through the two fat booklets provided for the population conference. There are hundreds of sessions on many different aspects of the subject. But there seems to be little relating to a global population explosion. Are these researchers living in a bubble? Don't they hear the raised voices of concern outside their discipline?

As I continue looking, I'm relieved to see that from midweek onwards there are some sessions on the link between population and environment.

But for the moment, the issue of 'total fertility rate'—that is how many children women have during the span of their reproductive lives—seems to be the focus of attention.

Since the 1970s fertility has declined considerably, not just in countries like Morocco but worldwide. This makes for a global average of around 2.5 children per woman.

In 76 countries the fertility rate has actually sunk below replacement level—which is set at around 2.1. This means that the current population is not reproducing itself. It's most noticeable in Europe but there are examples from every continent, including Africa.

In developing countries the average fertility rate fell by half, from six to three children, between 1950 and 2000. But in many countries of sub-Saharan and western Africa, women are still having five or more children on average.

In terms of the big global numbers, what happens in India and China, the two most populous countries, has the greatest impact. India today has a fertility rate of 2.7 (down from 3.5 in 1997) and is expected to hit replacement level in 2027. China's drop from 5 or 6 per woman before 1970 to around

1.5 today, looks likely to persist. 'The accumulated evidence suggests that lifting the one child policy would not lead to a resurgence of uncontrollable population growth,' say researchers from the region. China, they say, 'would benefit from learning from its neighbours, Korea and Japan, how difficult it is to induce people to increase childbearing once fertility has fallen to a very low level. As a consequence, China's population should start shrinking by 2023.

According to the United Nations, 21 countries already had a declining population in the period 2000–2005.

Contraceptive Use Is Credited

The rapid extension of family planning and contraceptive use around the world is to thank for this decline in fertility. Population worriers make much of the projection of nine billion by 2050. But were it not for three decades of successful family planning that figure would be closer to 16 billion, points out Australian demographer Peter McDonald.

Here in Morocco, for example, only five per cent of women used contraception in the late 1970s—today 63 per cent do. But another crucial factor is the progress made in getting girls into school. This, more than anything, delays childbearing, encourages greater spacing between children or even opens out the option of not having children at all.

It's the perfect chicken and egg. Education means lower fertility—and lower fertility can mean more education. One of the immediate benefits of the so-called 'demographic dividend' that comes with fewer children being born is that school rolls fall, educational resources are not so over-stretched, and there is, in theory at any rate, more money available per child for education. In practice, the money may be wasted or misdirected. But in South Korea, for example, where the demographic dividend was invested in education, the results in terms of economic and social development over the past few decades have been astounding.

The same felicitous connection exists between health provision and fertility rates. Statistically, a child's chance of survival improves hugely in a smaller family where resources—both physical and emotional—tend to be more concentrated. And if children have a better chance of surviving, their parents will not feel they need to have so many. This is one of the reasons why in countries where there is the greatest poverty—those of sub-Saharan Africa, for example—women both have the most children and lose the most children as infants.

Population Growth Is Stabilizing

At lunch I get talking with a researcher from Italy, which (at 1.3) has the lowest fertility rate in western Europe. She tells me: 'The traditional idea of motherhood is still very strong in Italy. Modern women who work and have careers don't want to be sucked into all that. They do not get enough support from either the state or their partners, to be able to work and have children.'

In Japan too a growing number of women are childless, hence a national fertility rate of just 1.2.

Young Japanese women are better educated than their mothers and have more career opportunities. In spite of this, traditional, patriarchal family values prevail. Though there is a 'departure from marriage' and a third of marriages end in divorce, cohabitation is still frowned upon, as is having children out of wedlock. The rate of celibacy is high for both sexes, compared with the West.

In South Korea the taboo against unmarried women having children is so strong that the overwhelming majority seek abortion or adoption. A woman who chooses to go ahead with a pregnancy and, worse still, keep her child is socially ostracized. She may lose her job, be rejected by her family and will be denied state benefits available to other parents.

Despite such harsh attitudes towards single mothers, policymakers in the region are getting anxious about falling fertil-

A History of Population Alarmism

With the population still growing by about 80 million each year, it's hard not to be alarmed. . . . Decades from now, there will likely be two billion more mouths to feed, mostly in poor countries. There will be billions more people wanting and deserving to boost themselves out of poverty. If they follow the path blazed by wealthy countries—clearing forests, burning coal and oil, freely scattering fertilizers and pesticides—they too will be stepping hard on the planet's natural resources. How exactly is this going to work?

There may be some comfort in knowing that people have long been alarmed about population. From the beginning, says French demographer Hervé Le Bras, demography has been steeped in talk of the apocalypse. Some of the field's founding papers were written just a few years after [Dutch scientist Antoni van] Leeuwenhoek's discovery [of microorganisms in the 1670s] by Sir William Petty, a founder of the Royal Society. He estimated that world population would double six times by the Last Judgment, which was expected in about 2,000 years. At that point it would exceed 20 billion people—more, Petty thought, than the planet could feed. "And then, according to the prediction of the Scriptures, there must be wars, and great slaughter, etc.," he wrote.

As religious forecasts of the world's end receded, Le Bras argues, population growth itself provided an ersatz mechanism of apocalypse. "It crystallized the ancient fear, and perhaps the ancient hope, of the end of days," he writes.

Robert Kunzig,
National Geographic, *January 2011.*

ity. According to Noriko Tsuya of Japan's Keio University: 'The new Government is promising to beef up child allowance by 2.5 times but so far attempts to encourage people to have children are not really helping.'

The anxiety is partly fuelled by national, cultural, psychological fears. 'A population in decline suggests decay,' observes demographer Paul Demeny of the Population Council, a leading research NGO [nongovernmental organization]. 'It is associated with the collapse of ancient civilizations.' Perhaps a smaller population will reduce a country's clout on the world stage, the thinking goes. Or it might slow down economic growth.

But even Japan's pronounced fertility decline is 'far from cataclysmic', according to Demeny. The country's population is set to dip from 127 to 102 million in 2050—still higher than its 1950 figure of 82 million.

For Demeny the global trend towards falling fertility means 'we are moving towards negative rates of growth, and stabilization at a lower population size. A lower population will lessen ecological footprints.'

But how does that tally with growing numbers of people in the world? Remember that median projection of nine billion by 2050?

One effect of falling fertility is that our current population growth is temporary. According to the UN projections, world population peaks in the latter half of the century at about 9.2 billion, then declines and stabilizes. That's not to brush aside environmental concerns or the need to treat population projections with caution. But it does put into perspective the alarmist claims of runaway population growth.

> "Ecological destruction and global poverty are intimately linked to overpopulation. But that topic seems almost taboo. It's a taboo we need to shatter."

The Taboo of Discussing Overpopulation Must Be Broken

Tom Flynn

While discussions about population control have taken place since the late eighteenth and early nineteenth centuries when British scholar Thomas Malthus first hypothesized that famine and disease would be two factors limiting runaway population growth, there is some question as to whether current debates on the issue fully address the supposedly dire and imminent consequences of current growth trajectories. In the following viewpoint, Tom Flynn resolutely answers that contemporary discussion of population growth is not taken seriously enough and that, until it is, current problems relating to the environment and poverty will not be solved. According to Flynn, environmental degradation and poverty are both "per capita" problems that manifest when there are too many people within a given area, in this case, on the planet. As such, unless the taboo about openly

Tom Flynn, "An Unfruitful Plea," *Free Inquiry*, vol. 29, December 2008–January 2009. Copyright ©2008 by the Council for Secular Humanism.

discussing overpopulation is broken, these problems will continue to plague societies worldwide. Tom Flynn is the editor of Free Inquiry, *the bimonthly publication of the Council for Secular Humanism.*

As you read, consider the following questions:

1. What does Flynn suggest is the optimum population, which the world census should be reduced to?

2. As stated by the author, how many times larger is a newborn's lifetime carbon footprint if it is born in the United States or United Kingdom as opposed to Ethiopia?

3. What does Flynn suggest that couples of childbearing age do in response to current population growth?

In his editorial ("The Two Imperatives of Planetary Ethics") [American philosophy professor, author, and leader in the US skeptic community] Paul Kurtz emphatically calls for secular humanists—and humans generally—to take action against oceanic dead zones and global poverty. Coastal-water eutrophication [introduction of substances not found naturally in the ecosystem] leads a grim lineup of ecological threats: global warming; freshwater depletion; and contamination by antibiotic residues, synthetic chemicals, and heavy metals, to name only a few. So ominous has the situation become that even many Christian conservatives are redefining themselves as stewards of the planet, no longer as its exploiters by divine right. As for poverty, its toll is inarguable, especially when we reflect that some two billion people, approximately the total population of planet Earth in 1942 when the original [antihunger organization] Oxfam was founded, live on $2 a day or less.

I chose that statistic because it points up a factor that Kurtz's ethical imperatives share, one that's too seldom discussed today. Both ecological destruction and global poverty are intimately linked to overpopulation. But that topic seems almost taboo.

It's a taboo we need to shatter.

A World of Per-Capita Problems

From the overuse of fertilizers that drives eutrophication to the carbon loading that drives global warming, most of the hazards threatening our biosphere are per-capita problems: they would be less oppressive if there were fewer people. Poverty and malnutrition have per-capita aspects as well: the green revolutions of the 1960s and 70s would have provided bountiful nutrition for all if third-world populations had not surged in response—driven as much by reduction in death rates as by increases in births. Since the desperately poor contribute little to their countries' GNPs [gross national products, the income produced from the sale of goods and services], it follows that rickety third-world economies would not be significantly smaller today if national populations had grown less explosively. Were that the case, the same modest resources could be distributed among fewer claimants, potentially reducing poverty.

The last time *Free Inquiry* ran a cover feature on overpopulation (August/September 2004, "What Is the Optimum Population of the U.S.? The World?"), I offered the controversial suggestion that humanity should seek over the long term to reduce its numbers to around 2.5 billion, the global population of the 1950s. Many who find that idea too radical nonetheless agree that we should seek to keep human numbers from overshooting the current 6.7 billion any farther than can be avoided. And, in fact, there are grounds for hope: most Western countries are now in a process of voluntary demographic contraction (the average German woman has just 1.3 children). Even in the United States, population would stabilize at current levels if not for immigration. Sadly, the response of Western leaders has been not to welcome falling birthrates but to resist them, offering childbirth bounties or soliciting new streams of immigrants.

Academics Speak Out

You wouldn't know it from the headlines, but there's a growing consensus among population experts that present population levels are ecologically unsustainable, not just in the third world but in developed countries like the United States and the United Kingdom (where each newborn's lifetime carbon footprint is some 160 times larger than that of an infant in Ethiopia).

That's why a July 2008 editorial in the *British Medical Journal* (the U.K. analogue of *The New England Journal of Medicine* or *JAMA*) is so welcome. Physicians John Guillebaud and Pip Hayes noted that there are 6.7 billion humans and that "humankind's consumption of fossil fuels, fresh water, crops, fish and forest exceeds supply. These facts are connected." Since the days of [British political scholar] Thomas Malthus [who wrote extensively on the impact of population increases], a "sevenfold increase in the population has led . . . to unprecedented food shortages, escalating prices, and riots. Until these events [American agronomist Norman] Borlaug's 'green revolution' had seemingly proved Malthus wrong. Yet fertilisers, pesticides, tractors, and transport are dependent on fossil fuels, which apart from being in short supply, exacerbate climate change."

Noting that recent *British Medical Journal* editorials on climate change had been silent about population, Guillebaud and Hayes asked, "Should UK doctors break a deafening silence here? . . . Should we now explain to UK couples who plan a family that stopping at two children, or at least having one less child than first intended, is the simplest and biggest contribution anyone can make to leaving a habitable planet for our grandchildren?"

Humans Can Solve the Overpopulation Problem

As far as we know there is only one species in the universe capable of conceptualizing its impact on its habitat. That's us. . . .

Today we face the challenge of solving the definitive human riddle. We are aware that we have an impact on the environment. We are aware that our population has been growing exponentially. We are aware that no species can expand infinitely on this finite planet. With this awareness comes responsibility.

We are capable of moderating our impact on the planet. We are capable of conceptualizing a sustainable human habitat and executing a plan to create that habitat.

Bryan Welch,
Mother Earth News, *April/May 2009.*

Kudos to Drs. Guillebaud and Hayes for their forthrightness and, yes, courage for posing these tough questions in the U.K.'s premier medical journal. (Care to guess the odds that any such viewpoint will soon appear in the *New England Journal of Medicine*)?

Speaking frankly about overpopulation need not raise the specter of coercive practices associated with some "population control" efforts of decades past, Guillebaud and Hayes note. It's been repeatedly demonstrated that simple education and advocacy concerning contraception suffice to reduce fecundity when "accompanied by correct information about its appropriateness and safety; when barriers are removed; and when the principles of marketing are applied."

Individuals Can Make a Difference

You don't need to be a physician to call attention to the links between environmental degradation, poverty, and overpopulation. Secular humanists should be outspoken on this score whenever opportunity presents. Those of childbearing age might also consider leading by example and having one fewer child—even if their doctor fails to recommend it.

Personally, I've been a population activist for many years. I long ago decided to be part of the solution, not part of the problem, and simply resolved not to have children. It's a decision I have never regretted—and yes, I know that dire consequences would ensue if everyone followed my lead. (Fat chance of that.) So long as some couples insist on having many children, we need others who will make the voluntary choice to have none. Look at it this way: by not having the two children a zero-population-growth commitment would "entitle" us to, my wife and I have made up for two thirds of the runaway fruitfulness of Todd and Sarah Palin.

Humor aside, it seems society is finally ready to get serious about what Kurtz has called "our common abode." Getting serious about the planet means getting serious about human numbers. Or we're not really being serious at all.

> *"If you follow the overpopulation argument to its logical conclusion, the solution to environmental crisis is one of two things—at best keeping countries like China in underdeveloped poverty, or at worst, advocating genocide."*

Discussions of Overpopulation Often Lead to Racist and Elitist Solutions

Andrew Cheeseman

The problem of overpopulation is often framed as a defining issue faced by humanity, with its solution being essential to the continued survival of the planet and all the species that inhabit it. In the viewpoint that follows, however, Andrew Cheeseman argues that the problem of overpopulation is a construct of capitalism that leads to racism and misleads people into blaming others instead of the capitalist system itself as the root problem. This deception, Cheeseman contends, focuses on human consumption as the cause of environmental destruction and leads to the conclusion that maintaining a small population of humans on the planet would mitigate this problem. According to the author, controlling the population would result in the consignment

Andrew Cheeseman, "Overpopulation: A Racist Myth," *Socialist Alternative*, April 26, 2007. Reproduced by permission.

of certain populations to lives of poverty or the complete eradication of those populations, both solutions that are steeped in racism. Andrew Cheeseman is a regular contributor to the Socialist Alternative, an Australian collective that promotes a socialist revamping of society.

As you read, consider the following questions:

1. As stated by Cheeseman, why is the environment a crucial question for socialists?

2. According to the author, to whom did Thomas Mathus's "solution" to overpopulation apply?

3. Why is the overpopulation argument "simply wrong," according to Cheeseman?

There's no doubt whatsoever that the earth's environment is in a terrible state. Even [former vice president] Al Gore accepts that global warming is a reality. Devastating, extreme weather (such as drought, floods, cyclones and hurricanes) is becoming more frequent, and scientists predict that this century will be worse. Polar icecaps are melting, and according to research carried out by Thomas R. Knutson of the US National Oceanic and Atmospheric Administration, global warming will cause the frequency of Category 5 hurricanes (the most powerful type) to double this century.

The environment is a crucial question for socialists. It's crucial because workers and the poor will suffer the most as the environment worsens—witness Hurricane Katrina for proof of this. And it's crucial because many of the strategies proposed to save our planet serve only to defend the system that is killing it—the system of capitalism.

So why is our planet in such a sorry state? One of the most common arguments is that there are simply too many people on the planet for nature to handle—that with six billion people on the planet, the environment cannot be saved.

However, the last 200 years have shown two crucial facts about the overpopulation argument—firstly that it is a conservative argument that leads to racism, and secondly that it is just plain wrong.

Promoting Poverty and Genocide

The "overpopulation" argument is much older than most realise. It was first advanced by [British political scholar] Thomas Malthus, who argued over 200 years ago that increasing world population would cause scarcity, starvation and environmental devastation within the 19th century, and that the world couldn't possibly produce enough food for one billion people. Malthus's "solution" was for efforts to be made to reduce birth rates and living standards—but only those of the poor and/or "undesirable".

In other words, rich whites could consume all they liked, while those poor or coloured enough to earn Malthus's contempt would suffer. Today, theories of overpopulation cause people to blame populous countries like China for environmental destruction—when the USA, with 78 per cent fewer people than China, uses 78 per cent more energy, and, according to the International Energy Agency, creates over 60 per cent more greenhouse gases.

If you follow the overpopulation argument to its logical conclusion, the solution to environmental crisis is one of two things—at best keeping countries like China in underdeveloped poverty, or at worst, advocating genocide.

Overpopulation in Defense of Capitalism

The overpopulation argument, however, is simply wrong. It ignores the fact that environmental damage is caused not in meeting human needs, but in maximising profits. Under capitalism, production is based upon profit, not the needs of humanity. As a result, corporations often ignore the environ-

Racist Motives Drive Anti-immigrant Environmentalism

Immigrants' rights proponents say the idea of tackling environmental issues via immigration controls is, at best, a misguided belief that ecological issues can be addressed within national borders in our global world, and at worst, a "greening of hate," wherein immigrants become scapegoats for a host of ills caused by Americans' own overconsumption and ill-conceived foreign policies. They say anti-immigration groups or activists with few bona fide environmentalist credentials appear to be using environmental arguments as a way to further agendas that are actually seated in racism.

Vicki Cervantes, a longtime Latin America solidarity activist based in Chicago, is afraid that in some cases, dedicated environmentalists who may not fully understand the immigration issue are being manipulated by those with a veiled xenophobic agenda.

Kari Lydersen, Earth Island Journal, *Summer 2009.*

mental impact of their actions—and the competitive nature of capitalism forces them to do just this, or to be undercut by less scrupulous competitors.

Even as early as the 1800s, obvious environmental damage was being caused by unsustainable farming methods used to squeeze every possible dollar out of the land. To quote [German socialist philosopher Karl] Marx's collaborator Frederick Engels:

"What cared the Spanish planters in Cuba who burned down forests on the slopes of the mountains and obtained from the ashes sufficient fertiliser for one generation of very highly profitable coffee trees—what cared they that the heavy tropical rainfall afterwards washed away the unprotected upper stratum of the soil, leaving behind only bare rock!"

During the 20th century, this drive for profit at any cost led to car companies (famously General Motors in America) purchasing public transport systems and running them into the ground—to boost car sales and profits. The same logic leads today to oil and coal power being used instead of clean, but less profitable alternatives like solar and wind power. And in the recent war in Lebanon—a war caused by the logic of capitalism—Israeli bombs caused the biggest oil slick since the [oil tanker] *Exxon Valdez* disaster of 1989.

The world isn't dying, it's being killed. Not by people like you and me, but by a mad economic system that puts the relentless quest for profits above everything else. As long as the quest for short-term profit is the most important driving force in society—as long as we live under capitalism—the environment will suffer. And arguments about overpopulation merely serve to defend this system, by telling ordinary people to blame ourselves and each other, rather than fighting back against the system that is destroying our planet and our future.

Periodical and Internet Sources Bibliography

The following articles have been selected to supplement the diverse views presented in this chapter.

Economist	"Go Forth and Multiply a Lot Less," October 31, 2009.
Alison George	"7 Billion and Counting . . . ," *New Scientist*, September 26, 2009.
Leo Hickman	"Can a Finite Planet Cope with Its Population Explosion?," *CCPA Monitor*, March 2011.
Charles Kenny	"Bomb Scare," *Foreign Policy*, May/June 2010.
Robert Kunzig	"By 2045 Global Population Is Projected to Reach Nine Billion. Can the Planet Take the Strain?," *National Geographic*, January 2011.
Jan Narveson	"Overpopulation? No Way!," *Free Inquiry*, April/May 2009.
David Nicholson-Lord	"Planet Overload," *New Statesman*, March 9, 2009.
Mark Rowe	"Safety in Numbers?," *Geographical*, August 2010.
Julia Whitty	"The Last Taboo," *Mother Jones*, May/June 2010.

What Problems Might Be Attributed to Population Growth?

Chapter Preface

Long before Paul Ehrlich made his twentieth-century predictions about the looming crisis attending overpopulation, eighteenth-century British scholar Thomas Malthus warned of similar dire consequences resulting from unabated population growth. Malthus's 1798 publication *An Essay on the Principle of Population* focused on the ways in which food shortages and disease outbreaks would limit continual increases in human numbers worldwide. Throughout the centuries since, his work has served as a cornerstone for population studies, specifically in relation to food and resource shortages, two of the largest problems blamed on the increasing human population.

However, many within academia view Malthus's predictions as outdated in the face of the myriad technological advances humans have made to counter many of the problems he predicted. Writing in *Scientific American* in 2008, American economist Jeffrey D. Sachs recalls the disdain with which his economics professors addressed Malthusian forecasts. He states, "For 200 years economists have dismissed Malthus for overlooking technological advancement," and goes on to contend that these arguments are predicated on the understanding that food shortages, for example, no longer threaten to wipe out humanity because, as a result of "advances in seed breeding, chemical fertilizers, irrigation, mechanization and more, the food supply can stay well ahead of the population curve." In addition to limitations in food production, economists have argued that improvements in health care and family planning, widespread urbanization, and economic growth have all limited the negative impacts that would supposedly accompany ongoing population increases.

While there has been a tendency to dismiss Malthus's predictions in some circles, the 2008 food crisis has reinvoked the specter of his overpopulation warnings. Stuart Harridge, who teaches international studies at Mazenod College in Melbourne, Australia, wrote in a 2009 issue of the journal *Ethos* that "the bleak vision of Thomas Malthus of a world where population growth outstripped food production, resulting in widespread famine and social chaos . . . after nearly 200 years, appears to have had some merit after all." Harridge concedes that hunger increased in 2007 and 2008 not as a result of too little food produced, as Malthus predicted, but rather due to insufficient food distribution channels; still, he maintains that the world's predicted population growth to more than 9 billion by mid-century remains a pressing problem requiring immediate attention from the global community. He concludes, "The global food crisis is not the fulfillment of Malthus's prophecy. It is, however, a warning."

Just as the predictions of Malthus continue to ring in the ears of those who have heard them, so too do the connections between overpopulation and numerous problems troubling the world today reverberate throughout society. Even economists such as Sachs, who was educated in a system that viewed Malthusian concerns about overpopulation as mistaken, still believe that these predictions warrant some attention and question whether they could come true. Sachs writes, "Have we beaten Malthus? Two centuries after his work, we still do not really know." The debate about the link between population increases and problems such as environmental degradation, hunger, and economic downturn continues in the following chapter as the authors wrestle with the question of what problems might be attributed to population growth.

> *"The faster our population increases, the sooner we use up . . . resources, and thus, the greater the impacts of global warming on our environment."*

Population Growth Is a Threat to the Environment

John and Mary Ellen Harte

In the viewpoint that follows, John and Mary Ellen Harte state their opinions about the ways in which environmental problems are worsened by the combined effects of population size, affluence, and technology. They argue that while each of these factors impacts environmental degradation, population size has the largest net impact as it combines with and exacerbates existing problems. The authors examine a variety of scenarios in which population size acts as a tipping point pushing environmental factors over a threshold, combines with other existing factors to multiply the existing negative environmental impacts of a situation, and works in a feedback loop amplifying already threatening situations. They warn that left unchecked, these compound systems can create intensified negative environmental and societal outcomes. John Harte is a professor of ecosystem sciences at the University of California–Berkeley, and Mary Ellen Harte is a biologist; together, they recently coauthored the book Cool the Earth, Save the Economy.

As you read, consider the following questions:

1. What equation do the authors use to express the environmental impact of population, affluence, and technology?

2. According to the Hartes, trees exposed to air pollutants might be more susceptible to what?

3. In addition to thresholds, synergies, and feedbacks, what factors do the authors identify as causing population growth to have "outsized effects" on the environment?

There were already twenty or so university students crowded around the TV, craning to see the electoral results flowing in on that fateful November day in 2008. But then a few more guests arrived, and as people politely jostled and made room, someone inevitably backed into a family treasure, which then crashed to the ground and broke. Yes, this really did happen to us—but it's actually a good allegory to the unusually important effects that even small increases in population can have on an already crowded planet. So many natural processes create linear, proportional consequences, and most people assume the same is true for the effects of our increasing population. But there are also plenty of examples of natural processes that create abrupt changes, once a threshold has been reached. The boiling point of water signals its abrupt change from liquid to gas. A magnifying glass can focus sunlight onto a piece of paper until it heats to its burning point, when it lights up in flames and quickly reduces to ashes. This would be totally unpredictable to someone ignorant of the burning threshold of paper, and of how magnifying glasses function.

Similarly, our ignorance of the web of existing natural thresholds means that we cannot often predict when seemingly small increases in population will cause catastrophic environmental changes, or set the trigger for such catastrophes through the unconscious crossing of natural thresholds. Given this, how *does* current population growth create environmental effects well beyond expected changes?

Myriad Links

A little context is needed here. For the past several centuries, humanity has been polluting air and water, altering Earth's climate, eliminating the habitat of plants and animals, and depleting the natural bank account of nonrenewable resources. Further, we are decreasing the capacity of natural ecosystems to regenerate or maintain renewable resources and "ecosystem services," such as providing clean air, water, fertile soil, flood control, an adequate climate, and the conservation of biological diversity. This is the environment in which our planetary population continues to grow.

The links between human activity and environmental degradation are myriad. But the human factors that contribute to environmental destruction can be grouped into three useful categories: population size (P), the individual rate of energy and material consumption that contribute to our affluence (A), and the impacts stemming from technologies (T), used to fuel that individual consumption rate. Their environmental impact (I) is often expressed as I=PAT.

Although a useful reminder that population, affluence and technology contribute environmental impacts, if taken too literally, the I=PAT equation can feed the illusion that, with affluence and technology remaining unchanged, proportional or linear increases in population cause proportional or linear environmental impacts. But this ignores a host of threshold effects, synergies, feedbacks, and other nonlinear phenomena that can amplify the environmental impact of human numbers. In reality, population size plays a much more dynamic and complex role in shaping environmental quality.

The Threshold Impact

A threshold is a phenomenon in which a small stress to a system generates little or no impact, but when the stress exceeds a certain (threshold) level, the impact increases dramatically. The response of surface waters to acid rain is an environmental example. Below the threshold, water alkalinity prevents lake acidification. But just beyond a threshold—where all the alkalinity has been used up, buffering previous acidic additions—the water acidity increases dramatically. Thus, quite suddenly, lakes can acidify, losing their ability to sustain life after a small addition of acid rain.

But the story gets much more complex. Fossil fuel combustion produces the acidity, so some urge that we switch to clean renewable energy sources, such as wind and solar power. But the limited availability of easily accessible clean energy creates an availability threshold. The faster population increases, the more quickly this threshold is reached, beyond which the population must increase its use of fossil fuels. In I=PAT terms, T (technologies) temporarily change as solar and wind sources replace some of the fossil fuel combustion. But the simultaneous increase in P (population size) quickly reaches the limits of new available technology, forcing a change back to fossil fuels. The real point is that P forces a change in T, so P is not a simple multiplier, but affects other multipliers as well.

Thresholds abound in nature. In Amazonia, where roughly a quarter of the rainforest has been destroyed, numerous species have gone extinct because their habitat became either too small or too fragmented to sustain them, or was initially so small and unique that it disappeared entirely. In both cases, thresholds were crossed. Virtually all ecological models predict that the rate of species extinction will increase faster than the incremental spatial loss of habitat. A threshold relationship also characterizes the epidemic spread of viruses in a dense population, be it human, animal, or plant monocultures, i.e., crops. The innate complexity of a system can sometimes make it impossible to predict a threshold. For example, it is difficult to predict what level of global heating will cause Greenlandic and Antarctic ice to greatly accelerate their melting, resulting in a rapid, dangerous rise in sea level. We know the threshold exists, however, even if we can't predict it.

Synergy of Population and Environment

Synergy occurs when the combined effect of two causes is greater than the sum of the effects of each cause acting separately from each other. Clearly, if two environmental stresses act synergistically *and* each stress grows proportionately with population size, then the combined effect of both may grow faster with population size than just linearly.

Imagine you are in a room with two doors allowing escape, and a poisonous gas is released into the room. If one door is locked, your escape out the other door may be delayed but you get out. Similarly, if it is only the second door that is locked, your delayed escape through the first is likely. But when both are locked, you are trapped. Something similar can happen in the biosphere when stresses act in concert.

Here's an example. Consider the separate and combined effects on biodiversity of climate change induced by fossil fuel burning, and land use practices leading to loss or fragmentation of forest habitat. Forest loss can force species to find adjacent intact forest habitat. Climate change can force species to migrate to cooler latitudes, or uphill to find suitable climate habitat. When the two stresses act together, the effect is worse than the sum of the effects of each stress acting separately, because migration can be impeded by habitat destruction.

But again, the problem is more complex. Deforestation can contribute to the problem of acid rain. In Africa, nitric acid is formed from burning vegetation. Our forest species, weakened by either a lack or degradation of suitable environment, becomes more vulnerable to other threats. For example, fish weakened by radiation have been shown to be more easily damaged by thermal pollution than are healthy fish, and trees subjected to some air pollutants become more susceptible to insect damage.

We noted above that a habitat can become too small or fragmented to sustain a species, but this is worsened disproportionately by an increase in human population size. How?

Consider a tale of three cities, which, with rising populations, become six. The original three were connected by three avenues of highways and transmission line rights-of-way, which are barriers to wildlife movement, death traps for some species, and opportunities for invasive species (that may displace native species) to spread. These avenues also fragmented the habitat into two pieces: inside and outside the triangle. With six cities, fifteen avenues now connect them, implying a fivefold increase in these harmful stresses on plants and animals, and the habitat is further fragmented into seventeen pieces: sixteen within the network of avenues, and the habitat outside it. While this is only a schematic, it does illustrate how the web of infrastructural interconnections in human society, which also becomes increasingly dense as population grows, can result in synergistic land-use effects that damage biodiversity.

Feedbacks Grow with Population

Another process that results in nonlinear amplification—feedback—occurs when a process results in changes that, in turn, affect the rate of the original process. It adds indirectly to the direct factors already driving the process. Feedbacks are abundant in the natural world and occur at all levels of complexity, from the global climate system and ecosystems to the genome of a cell.

Global warming is a good illustration of feedbacks at work. The buildup of greenhouse gases in the atmosphere is a direct cause of increased surface temperature, due to the extra heat-absorbing capacity of these gases. As models consistently show, this direct effect is roughly 2° Fahrenheit for a doubling of the greenhouse gas carbon dioxide. But this direct effect also triggers feedbacks. As ice and snow melt away under global warming, there are fewer white surfaces that reflect sunlight back to space. Without that reflective covering, more sunlight is absorbed by Earth's surface, heating it and accelerating global warming. This reinforcing effect is called a positive feedback. Positive feedbacks reinforcing existing environmental problems are prevalent and of increasing concern.

In some ecological processes, global warming feedbacks grow with human population size. For example, in a warmer climate, people may rely more on air conditioning, thereby burning more fossil fuels and emitting more carbon dioxide, causing a positive feedback. As warming creates drier conditions, wildfires will increase in frequency and intensity. Wildfires, in turn, release carbon dioxide to the atmosphere, creating yet another positive feedback on global warming.

There are several global warming feedbacks amplified by population that occur from agriculture. Warming is also likely to accelerate the decomposition of soil organic matter, particularly in tilled, fertilized, and irrigated soils. That decomposition in turn, will accelerate the release of carbon dioxide into the atmosphere. Because the total area of cultivated land increases with population size, population growth affects the intensity of this positive feedback. Hotter temperatures and increasing drought frequency and intensity from global warming increase the need for irrigation. Simultaneously, population growth increases global warming and the amount of land

and water needed to grow food. As a result, we will be forced into more energy-intensive technologies to obtain water and maintain our level of affluence, accelerating our emissions of carbon dioxide and, thus, global warming.

More Reasons for Outsized Effects

Beyond thresholds, synergies, and feedbacks, there is an assortment of other reasons for why population growth can have outsized effects on the environment. One is the "low-hanging fruit" phenomenon: just as low-hanging fruit gets picked first, human societies tend to use the most fertile soil, the cleanest water, and the least polluting fossil fuels first. As we use up these desirable resources, our options are increasingly limited to second-rate resources.

Another phenomenon is the exhaustion of natural processes that act as "sinks" for our pollutants. Each year, oceans and forests absorb carbon dioxide from the atmosphere, alleviating somewhat the problem of global warming. Currently, these ecosystems absorb about a third of this gas produced by humans, with a little over half going into the oceans. Because these carbon sinks have limits, they are nonrenewable resources, and can overflow if too much is put into them too fast. In fact, careful measurements show that oceans are slowing in their absorption of carbon dioxide. The faster our population increases, the sooner we use up these resources, and thus, the greater the impacts of global warming on our environment.

Similarly, when we deplete natural sources of clean water, either in aquifers or surface streams, we must turn to new technologies for water, and many of these, such as dams and desalinization, carry environmental costs.

An Intensifying Downward Spiral

Let's return to I=PAT and the global warming effect on irrigation. We described above how increasing population size (P) will force us to use new technologies (T) to get more irrigation water to grow the food that, in turn, maintains our afflu-ence (A). T can be considered a function of P, and vice versa. These two drivers cannot be disentangled.

When A and T are fixed, however, it's not just the magni-tude of environmental impacts, I, that increases dispropor-tionately with P, a point made when we first described I=PAT. Our efforts to solve social problems, such as environmental injustice arising from inequitable distribution of impacts and of resources across income, cultural and racial groups, are hindered by rapidly growing numbers. High rates of popula-tion growth make it more difficult to ensure adequate school-ing, material resources, and civic order, thereby worsening so-cial conditions. These effects form the subtext of everyday news. A recent *New York Times* article on abuse of servants in Pakistan, for example, observed that the country's population is growing far faster than its economy, creating more poverty that forces many to become miserable, slave-like servants.

In a pernicious feedback, these social problems make it more difficult to solve environmental problems. For example, in an equitable society with only small income disparities, a carbon tax to discourage fossil fuel consumption would make a great deal of sense. The tax burden would be distributed evenly, unlike in an inequitable society, where the poor spend a larger fraction of their income on fuel than do the rich. So, in an equitable society the carbon tax would not exacerbate inequality, but in an inequitable society it would. Thus, the population trap catches us twice, environmentally and socially. Growing populations exacerbate social problems, and growing social problems frustrate efforts to solve environmental prob-lems. Unsolved environmental problems further worsen injus-tice and inequity. What results is an intensifying downward spiral.

> *"Overpopulation is not driving environmental destruction at the global level; overconsumption is."*

Overconsumption, Not Overpopulation, Is a Threat to the Environment

Fred Pearce

In the following viewpoint, Fred Pearce argues that, contrary to those who believe that population increases are the root of environmental problems worldwide, overconsumption is in fact the main threat to the environment. Pearce traces the use of global resources by individuals in the United States to show that, in comparison with the rest of the world, Americans use proportionally more than their share of major commodities. Due to this discrepancy between American population size and consumption, Pearce maintains that even with the projected increases in population in the developing world, the resource use and carbon footprints of those in the Western world will continue to outpace those of individuals in the developing world. Thus, even if the population continues to increase in these countries, and Pearce gives evidence that this may not be the case, he maintains that

Fred Pearce,"Consumption Dwarfs Population as Main Environmental Threat," *Yale Environment 360*, April 13, 2009. Copyright © 2009. Reproduced by permission of the author.

the greatest strain on the environment comes in the form of Western resource consumption. Fred Pearce is a British journalist and author who consults for the magazine New Scientist *and has written the books* When the Rivers Run Dry, With Speed and Violence, *and* Confessions of an Eco-Sinner: Tracking Down the Sources of My Stuff.

As you read, consider the following questions:

1. As stated by the author, what percentage of the carbon dioxide emissions do the richest 7 percent of the world's population produce?

2. How does the average amount of land required for a typical American lifestyle compare with that of other countries, according to Pearce?

3. According to the statistics quoted by the author, how do the carbon emissions of an American child over his lifetime compare with those of children from China, Pakistan, India, and Nigeria?

It's the great taboo, I hear many environmentalists say. Population growth is the driving force behind our wrecking of the planet, but we are afraid to discuss it.

It sounds like a no-brainer. More people must inevitably be bad for the environment, taking more resources and causing more pollution, driving the planet ever farther beyond its carrying capacity. But hold on. This is a terribly convenient argument—"over-consumers" in rich countries can blame "over-breeders" in distant lands for the state of the planet. But what are the facts?

The world's population quadrupled to six billion people during the 20th century. It is still rising and may reach 9 billion by 2050. Yet for at least the past century, rising per-capita incomes have outstripped the rising head count several times over. And while incomes don't translate precisely into increased resource use and pollution, the correlation is distressingly strong.

Moreover, most of the extra consumption has been in rich countries that have long since given up adding substantial numbers to their population.

American Consumption Drains Resources

By almost any measure, a small proportion of the world's people take the majority of the world's resources and produce the majority of its pollution. Take carbon dioxide emissions—a measure of our impact on climate but also a surrogate for fossil fuel consumption. Stephen Pacala, director of the Princeton Environment Institute, calculates that the world's richest half-billion people—that's about 7 percent of the global population—are responsible for 50 percent of the world's carbon dioxide emissions. Meanwhile the poorest 50 percent are responsible for just 7 percent of emissions.

Although overconsumption has a profound effect on greenhouse gas emissions, the impacts of our high standard of living extend beyond turning up the temperature of the planet. For a wider perspective of humanity's effects on the planet's life support systems, the best available measure is the "ecological footprint," which estimates the area of land required to provide each of us with food, clothing, and other resources, as well as to soak up our pollution. This analysis has its methodological problems, but its comparisons between nations are firm enough to be useful.

They show that sustaining the lifestyle of the average American takes 9.5 hectares [one hectare equals 10,000 square meters; about 2.5 acres], while Australians and Canadians require 7.8 and 7.1 hectares respectively; Britons, 5.3 hectares; Germans, 4.2; and the Japanese, 4.9. The world average is 2.7 hectares. China is still below that figure at 2.1, while India and most of Africa (where the majority of future world population growth will take place) are at or below 1.0.

The United States always gets singled out. But for good reason: It is the world's largest consumer. Americans take the greatest share of most of the world's major commodities: corn, coffee, copper, lead, zinc, aluminum, rubber, oil seeds, oil, and natural gas. For many others, Americans are the largest per-capita consumers. In "super-size-me" land, Americans gobble up more than 120 kilograms of meat a year per person, compared to just 6 kilos in India, for instance.

I do not deny that fast-rising populations can create serious local environmental crises through overgrazing, destructive farming and fishing, and deforestation. My argument here is that viewed at the global scale, it is overconsumption that has been driving humanity's impacts on the planet's vital life-support systems during at least the past century. But what of the future?

The Global Economic Downturn

We cannot be sure how the global economic downturn will play out. But let us assume that [economist] Jeffrey Sachs, in his book *Common Wealth*, is right to predict a 600 percent increase in global economic output by 2050. Most projections put world population then at no more than 40 percent above today's level, so its contribution to future growth in economic activity will be small.

Of course, economic activity is not the same as ecological impact. So let's go back to carbon dioxide emissions. Virtually all of the extra 2 billion or so people expected on this planet in the coming 40 years will be in the poor half of the world. They will raise the population of the poor world from approaching 3.5 billion to about 5.5 billion, making them the poor two-thirds.

Sounds nasty, but based on Pacala's calculations—and if we assume for the purposes of the argument that per-capita emissions in every country stay roughly the same as today—those extra two billion people would raise the share of emissions contributed by the poor world from 7 percent to 11 percent.

Look at it another way. Just five countries are likely to produce most of the world's population growth in the coming decades: India, China, Pakistan, Nigeria, and Ethiopia. The carbon emissions of one American today are equivalent to those of around four Chinese, 20 Indians, 30 Pakistanis, 40 Nigerians, or 250 Ethiopians.

Even if we could today achieve zero population growth, that would barely touch the climate problem—where we need to cut emissions by 50 to 80 percent by mid-century. Given existing income inequalities, it is inescapable that overconsumption by the rich few is the key problem, rather than overpopulation of the poor many.

Consumption Differs Around the World

But, you ask, what about future generations? All those big families in Africa begetting yet-bigger families. They may not consume much today, but they soon will.

Well, first let's be clear about the scale of the difference involved. A woman in rural Ethiopia can have ten children and her family will still do less damage, and consume fewer resources, than the family of the average soccer mom in Minnesota or Munich. In the unlikely event that her ten children live to adulthood and have ten children of their own, the entire clan of more than a hundred will still be emitting less carbon dioxide than you or I.

And second, it won't happen. Wherever most kids survive to adulthood, women stop having so many. That is the main reason why the number of children born to an average woman around the world has been in decline for half a century now. After peaking at between 5 and 6 per woman, it is now down to 2.6.

This is getting close to the "replacement fertility level" which, after allowing for a natural excess of boys born and women who don't reach adulthood, is about 2.3. The UN expects global fertility to fall to 1.85 children per woman by mid-century. While a demographic "bulge" of women of child-bearing age keeps the world's population rising for now, continuing declines in fertility will cause the world's population to stabilize by mid-century and then probably to begin falling.

Far from ballooning, each generation will be smaller than the last. So the ecological footprint of future generations could diminish. That means we can have a shot at estimating the long-term impact of children from different countries down the generations.

The best analysis of this phenomenon I have seen is by Paul Murtaugh, a statistician at Oregon State University. He recently calculated the climatic "intergenerational legacy" of today's children. He assumed current per-capita emissions and UN fertility projections. He found that an extra child in the United States today will, down the generations, produce an eventual carbon footprint seven times that of an extra Chinese child, 46 times that of a Pakistan child, 55 times that of an Indian child, and 86 times that of a Nigerian child.

Of course those assumptions may not pan out. I have some confidence in the population projections, but per-capita emissions of carbon dioxide will likely rise in poor countries for some time yet, even in optimistic scenarios. But that is an issue of consumption, not population.

The Fallacy of the Lifeboat Argument

In any event, it strikes me as the height of hubris to downgrade the culpability of the rich world's environmental footprint because generations of poor people not yet born might one day get to be as rich and destructive as us. Overpopulation is not driving environmental destruction at the global level; overconsumption is. Every time we talk about too many babies in Africa or India, we are denying that simple fact.

At root this is an ethical issue. Back in 1974, the famous environmental scientist Garret Hardin proposed something he called "lifeboat ethics". In the modern, resource-constrained world, he said, "each rich nation can be seen as a lifeboat full of comparatively rich people. In the ocean outside each lifeboat swim the poor of the world, who would like to get in." But there were, he said, not enough places to go around. If any were let on board, there would be chaos and all would drown. The people in the lifeboat had a duty to their species to be selfish—to keep the poor out.

Hardin's metaphor had a certain ruthless logic. What he omitted to mention was that each of the people in the lifeboat was occupying ten places, whereas the people in the water only wanted one each. I think that changes the argument somewhat.

"*The impacts of the growing world population on land, water, energy, and biota resources are real and indeed overwhelming.*"

Population Growth Strains Nonrenewable Resources

David Pimentel and Marcia Pimentel

Global resources will continue to dwindle as population growth goes unchecked, argue David and Marcia Pimentel in the following viewpoint. The authors examine resources such as water, cropland, and oil that humans have been consuming at a fevered pace in recent years and present a picture of how the exhaustion of these nonrenewable commodities poses a great threat to human survival. The authors contend that as long as the global population continues to increase, the strain placed on these resources will likewise continue to increase, and without close supervision, this strain could result in a forced population decrease simply because there will be too few resources to sustain further growth. David Pimentel is an ecology and agricultural sciences professor at Cornell University, and Marcia Pimentel is a senior lecturer in Cornell's College of Human Ecology, Division of Nutritional Sciences.

David Pimentel and Marcia Pimentel, "The Real Perils of Human Population Growth," *Free Inquiry*, vol. 29, April–May 2009. Copyright ©2009 by the Council for Secular Humanism.

As you read, consider the following questions:

1. What percentage of the world's freshwater is used in agricultural production, as stated by the authors?

2. According to the Pimentels, what are some of the problems that accompany the production and use of biofuels?

3. By how much do the authors suggest that Americans must reduce their consumption of goods and energy?

About forty years ago, the world population was only 3.5 billion, or about half of the present population of 6.7 billion people. Most of us seem to ignore or be unaware of the magnitude of this rapid expansion and the vast changes that it is causing throughout the world. Indeed, the daily and even the annual impacts of this growth go unnoticed. Yet the impacts of the growing world population on land, water, energy, and biota resources are real and indeed overwhelming.

What resources are required to secure a quality life for future generations worldwide? Will there be sufficient cropland, water, energy, and biological resources to provide adequate food and other essential human needs? Balanced against the future availability of these basic resources are the escalating needs of an ever-growing population.

Food Availability Is Diminishing

Clear scientific evidence suggests worldwide problems of food availability already have emerged. According to the World Health Organization, nearly 60 percent of the world population now is malnourished—the largest number and proportion of malnourished people ever reported in history. Further, many serious diseases, like malaria, HIV/AIDS, and tuberculosis are increasing, not only because of worldwide malnutrition but also because the increasing density and movement of human populations facilitate the spread of diseases.

More humans than ever before cover the earth with their urbanization, highways, and other activities. This imperils the availability of land resources. Cropland is a vital resource, with more than 99.7 percent of human food calories coming from the land and less than 0.3 percent from oceans and other aquatic ecosystems. Globally, an average of only 0.22 hectares of cropland per capita is now available for crop production. In contrast, 0.5 hectares per capita is available to support the diverse food systems of the United States and Europe. At present, cropland in the United States now occupies 17 percent of the total land area, but relatively little additional cropland is available to support the future expansion of U.S. agriculture. As a result, valuable forest areas are being permanently destroyed and replaced with cropland. This is causing many long-range global problems, including contributing to global warming.

Each year more than 10 million hectares of valuable cropland are degraded and lost because of soil erosion. In addition, an added 10 million hectares are being destroyed by salinization resulting from improper irrigation. Combined, world soil erosion and salinization account for the major losses in productive cropland.

Along with the loss of cropland and irrigated land, per-capita fertilizer use worldwide is declining, and all these changes are suppressing food-crop production, especially in developing countries. Adding to the 22 percent decline in per-capita use of fertilizers is the rapid increase in fertilizer prices. This decline is a concern because fertilizer nutrients are critical for crop production. The recent doubling of fertilizer prices had major impacts on farmers, especially struggling farmers in developing countries.

The major changes now occurring in world cereal-grain production should alert us to the problems ahead. Cereal grains comprise about 80 percent of the world's human food intake, making their sustained availability vital to human survival. Disturbing reports from the United Nations Food and Agriculture Organization indicate per-capita availability of basic cereal grains has been decreasing for the past twenty-four years. Thus far, despite all the advances in biotechnology and agricultural technologies, per-capita grain production has continued a slow decline since 1984, as harvests have to be divided among an increasing number of people.

Declining Water Supplies

Cropland without adequate water is unproductive. Adequate quantities of freshwater, which support the very survival of every human, plant, and animal on Earth, are not available in many regions of the world. A human requires slightly more than one liter of water each day. In contrast, producing the food needed to feed a human each day requires more than 1,600 liters of water.

Indeed, more than 70 percent of all available freshwater is used in world agriculture. For example, to produce one hectare of corn requires 5 million liters of water during the growing season (more than 600,000 gallons per acre). Further, the 17 percent of arid cropland that is now irrigated provides about 40 percent of the world's food. This confirms the importance of water and the role of irrigation in world food production.

As human populations continue to increase, more freshwater will be required for consumption by people, crops, and livestock. Water is being removed in some aquifers in the Western United States ten times faster than the recharge rate. Existing water conflicts within and between countries will escalate.

Depleted Energy Supplies

Over time, energy from many sources has assisted humans in their activities, from growing crops to sustaining major transportation systems. Prior to 1850, Americans were primarily dependent on forests for their fuel. Today, Americans are 96 percent dependent on fossil energy. Nearly 20 percent of all the fossil energy used in the United States is devoted to supplying food. In the last century, agriculture in industrialized nations has used enormous quantities of fossil energy to produce fertilizers and pesticides, to manufacture and run farm machinery, and to power irrigation systems. All of these fossil-energy based additions to agricultural production have greatly increased total energy requirements. For example, to produce one hectare of corn or rice currently requires approximately 1,000 liters of oil equivalents. But in contrast, in developing countries, expensive fossil energy has been replaced by human and animal power in order to provide the needed energy for crop production. About 1,200 hours of human manual labor are required to produce a hectare of grain.

Americans hold the dubious honor of being the world's leaders in fossil energy use. An average American consumes about 9,500 liters of gasoline energy-equivalents each year. Because of this high fossil-energy use and inadequate domestic energy sources, the United States now imports nearly 70 percent of its oil at an annual cost of $700 billion.

Yes, oil is a finite energy resource. The world supply of oil has peaked, and the remaining oil will now decline as use continues. Reliable projections are that by 2040 the world supply of oil will be more than 60 percent depleted. As oil resources diminish worldwide, costs increase, as evidenced until the current economic slowdown.

In the United States, supplies of natural gas and coal are expected to last fifty to one hundred years, depending on how fast they are substituted for oil and how fast the U.S. population grows. However, the processing of coal into oil and gas will contribute to damaging air pollution and global climate change unless technology is developed to help overcome these serious consequences.

Currently, the U.S. population uses about 100 quads of energy each year. (A quad is a large unit equivalent to 10^{15} BTUs [i.e., a quadrillion British thermal units].) This rate of consumption will continue to increase as the population continues to grow and further diminish fossil energy reserves. Now, as world fossil-energy sources are being depleted, all renewable energy sources must be investigated and priority given to their development and use. Depending on the geographic region, the most reliable of the potential renewable sources are wind power, photovoltaics, solar, thermal, and biomass energy. Even if all of these solar-based technologies become fully operational, they are projected to provide only about half—of the current U.S. consumption of fossil energy—or nearly 50 quads of energy. Furthermore, these renewable energy sources would occupy another 17 percent of additional land area, mostly in order to collect the solar energy. Some of this required land would compete with vital cropland, pasture, and forest land. Nuclear energy will probably have to be developed further in the world. At present, France has one of the better models for the relatively safe use of nuclear energy.

Biofuels Worsen Existing Problems

Optimists suggest ethanol produced from corn grain and cellulosic biomass, like grasses, could replace much of the oil used in United States. But consider that when 20 percent of the U.S. corn crop was converted into 6 billion gallons of ethanol in 2007, it replaced only 1 percent of U.S. oil consumption. If the entire corn crop were converted into ethanol, it would replace a mere 7 percent of oil consumption—and not make the United States independent of foreign oil! More critical is the fact that it takes 140 percent more fossil energy to produce one liter of ethanol than is contained in the ethanol produced.

Using food crops such as corn grain, canola, soybeans, and sugarcane to produce biofuels also causes major nutritional and economic concerns. Nearly 60 percent of humans in the world are currently malnourished, so the need for grains and other basic foods is critical. Jacques Diouf, director general of the U.N. Food & Agriculture Organization, reports that biofuel production is increasing human starvation worldwide. Therefore, growing crops for fuel squanders land, water, and energy resources vital for the production of food for people. The president of the World Bank reported that at peak, biofuels increased world food prices 75 percent.

Unfortunately, the environmental impacts of corn ethanol are serious and diverse. These include severe soil erosion of valuable cropland, the consumption of large amounts of water, plus the heavy use of costly nitrogen fertilizer and pesticides that pollute soils and waterways. In addition, large quantities of carbon dioxide are produced and released into the atmosphere because of the significant amounts of fossil-fuel energy that are needed in ethanol production. Then, during the subsequent fermentation process, about 25 percent of the carbon from the sugars and starches is released as carbon dioxide into the atmosphere, thereby contributing to global warming.

Cellulosic biomass is touted as the replacement for corn in making ethanol. Unfortunately, cellulosic biomass contains less than one-third the amount of starches and sugars found in corn and requires major fossil-energy inputs to release the more-tightly bound starches and sugars it contains for ethanol conversion. About 170 percent more energy (oil and gas) is required to produce ethanol from cellulosic biomass than in the ethanol produced.

The Human Toll

Over many decades, the pervasive use of chemicals throughout the world has expanded, impacting the survival of animals, plants, and microbes while also presenting serious constraints to ensuring sustainability. Exposure to a variety of chemicals is documented to contribute to a variety of serious human diseases. These include cancer, birth defects, immune system defects, reduced intelligence, behavioral abnormalities, decreased fertility, altered sex hormones, altered metabolism, and specific organ dysfunctions.

Air pollution, especially that caused by the increased burning of fossil fuels by humans, is predicted to have negative impacts on the environment. The widespread activities of agriculture, public health, and various aspects of the broader environment will suffer. Some problems and damages associated with global warming are already apparent, especially in agriculture. These changes include altered rainfall patterns, increased length of growing seasons, and increased pest problems.

Recent studies of environmental refugees throughout the world reveal their numbers are increasing. These movements of human populations contribute to major changes in population distribution and global insecurity. Understandably, these refugees are fleeing income disparity as well as shortages of food, cropland, freshwater, fossil energy, and other diverse essential resources they need for survival. This pattern will increase over time as the world population increases. According to the United Nations, the rapid growth in the world population serves as a potential breeding ground for terrorists and threatens global peace and security.

Population Continues to Grow

The present world population of 6.7 billion is projected by the United Nations to increase to 9 billion and may rise to as many as 11 billion by 2050. Even if a worldwide policy of two children per couple (instead of the current 2.8 children) were agreed on tomorrow, the world population will continue to expand for about seventy years before stabilizing at about *13*

Years Elapsed Between Major Milestones in Human Population Growth

Years Elapsed	Year	Approx. Population
3,000,000	10,000 BC (Agricultural Revolution)	5–10 million
10,000	AD 1	170 million
1,600	~1600	500 million
200	~1800 (Industrial Revolution)	1 billion
130	1930	2 billion
30	1960	3 billion
15	1975	4 billion
12	1987	5 billion
12	1999	6 billion
12	2011	7 billion

TAKEN FROM: William N. Ryerson, "Population: The Multiplier of Everything Else," Post Carbon Institute, 2010.

billion people. China, with a present policy of one child per couple, will add about 8 million to its population this year because of its young-age structure. Population momentum depends on the young-age structure of the current world population and propels the speed of growth. Note that 40 percent of the world population is under the age of twenty.

To be able to ensure a reasonable standard of living, Americans will have to reduce their population and their consumption of goods and energy by one-half. When the United States runs out of oil, natural gas, and coal, it will have to rely only on renewable energy. Such renewable energy sources will be able to provide only about half of the oil equivalents now used per capita each year—slightly more than 5,000 liters of oil equivalents instead of the current 9,500 liters per capita.

But as the population continues to grow and resources decline, several problems will increase.

Clearly, the current energy-population imbalance will impose drastic changes in energy, land, and water use and result in major changes in the American lifestyle. Achieving energy conservation and efficiency of all energy sources is paramount. Other major changes should include: smaller automobile size with double the gasoline efficiency; significant reductions in living space; reduction in heating, cooling, and light-energy usage; improvement in the movement of goods by energy-efficient methods; and heightened consumption of locally produced goods.

To halt the escalating imbalance between expanding population numbers and the earth's essential natural resources, humans must control their numbers. At the same time, they must make efforts to conserve cropland, freshwater, energy, biodiversity, and the other life-supporting environmental resources. People in developed countries could contribute by reducing their high consumption of all natural resources, especially fossil fuels.

Continued rapid population growth damages the lives of all individuals and their offspring. Personal well-being, based on health as well as personal freedoms, is directly related to population numbers. If humans do not control their numbers, nature will.

I "Worldwide food production has not
kept pace with population growth."

Global Population Growth Will Cause More Hunger

Commonweal

In most parts of the developing world, food security is no longer a daily concern for the population. However, there are still places where people must deal with the uncertainty of what, if anything, they will have to eat. In the following viewpoint, the editors of Commonweal *examine the increase in global hunger and argue that ongoing population increases combined with a variety of other factors including political, logistical and structural, and economic shortcomings have led to the current situation where one in six people go hungry worldwide. The authors see the successes of the "green revolution," which throughout the latter years of the twentieth century served as a solution to the starvation of the past, as short-lived and unsustainable. They urge international aid groups and national governments to work together to find a new, sustainable solution that can ensure no one goes hungry in the years to come.* Commonweal *is a Catholic magazine covering religious, political, and cultural issues.*

As you read, consider the following questions:

1. According to the UN numbers cited by the authors, how many starving people were there when the article was written in 2009?

2. What percentage of food does Africa import, as stated by *Commonweal*?

3. What do the authors identify as the problems with the large-scale farming methods championed during Norman Borlaug's Green Revolution?

When Norman Borlaug died last month [September 2009] at the age of ninety-five, the *Economist* called the Norwegian-American plant pathologist the "feeder of the world."

Borlaug's work dramatically improved wheat production, first in Mexico and then in Asia. It led to the "Green Revolution" of the 1960s and earned him the Nobel Peace Prize. In India alone, wheat production rose from 12 million tons in 1965 to 20 million tons in 1970, the year Borlaug won the prize. Unfortunately, his legacy may scarcely outlive him.

Since 1990, worldwide food production has not kept pace with population growth, and even farmers implementing Borlaug's methods (planting single crops reliant on the use of artificial fertilizers and pesticides) have seen their yields plateau and diminish. The UN now reports that there will be more starving people this year (individuals who will suffer acute hunger all year long) than ever before: 1.02 billion—one out of six human beings.

Population Growth and Politics

What happened? For one thing, population continued to grow. Add to that a lack of political will, logistical and structural failures, and the worldwide economic downturn. As a result, food prices rose significantly compared to people's income.

According to the UN, food prices are, on average, 25 percent higher than they were two years ago [in 2007]. Demand and energy costs will keep them there. The situation is aggravated by political instability in parts of the developing world, climate change, greater reliance on food imports, and stagnating wages. It is little wonder there have been food riots in Egypt, India, Haiti, and Latin America.

It is also apparent that the long-term effects of the vaunted neoliberal economic policies of the 1980s have come back to haunt us. The so-called structural adjustments foisted onto developing countries by both the World Bank and the International Monetary Fund put a premium on free trade and unfettered markets. But they failed to apply similar restrictions on government-subsidized agriculture in the West. This led to bountiful agribusiness profits but made the developing nations more reliant on imports and subject to sudden price fluctuations. Whereas Africa exported food in the 1960s, today it imports nearly 25 percent of what it consumes.

Perhaps the most succinct diagnosis of the situation was issued by Pope Benedict XVI last summer prior to the G-8 meeting [Group of Eight, forum for governments of eight major world economies] in Aquila, Italy. The problem of food scarcity, wrote Benedict in *Caritas in veritate* (no. 27), requires long-term solutions that eliminate "the structural causes that give rise to it." Promoting agricultural development can best be achieved "by investing in rural infrastructure, irrigation systems, transport, organization of markets, and in the development . . . of the human, natural, and socio-economic resources . . . available at the local level." According to Benedict, that is the surest course for guaranteeing sustainability over the long haul. At the G-8 meeting that followed, President Barack Obama convinced other leaders to pledge $20 billion over the next three years for sustainable agriculture in poor countries. The key, both he and the pope argued, is sustainability.

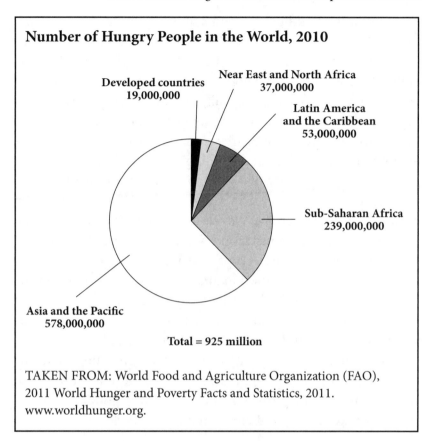

Number of Hungry People in the World, 2010

Developed countries
19,000,000

Near East and North Africa
37,000,000

Latin America
and the Caribbean
53,000,000

Sub-Saharan Africa
239,000,000

Asia and the Pacific
578,000,000

Total = 925 million

TAKEN FROM: World Food and Agriculture Organization (FAO), 2011 World Hunger and Poverty Facts and Statistics, 2011. www.worldhunger.org.

Allocating Aid to Stop Starvation

The great leap forward represented by Borlaug's Green Revolution was fleeting. It relied on large-scale farming methods more suitable to Kansas than to Kenya: huge tracts of arable land for single-crop cultivation; intensive fertilizer application; ever increasing use of pesticides; and vast quantities of available water. This approach met with initial success, but the price proved high. In areas like the Punjab (India's bread basket), outlays for seed, fertilizer, and transport soared, and the water table dropped alarmingly—more than two feet per year over the past five years alone. Such "development" was and will remain unsustainable.

International aid groups and some governments have come to the same realization. The Bill and Melinda Gates Foundation, for example, has spent $1.3 billion on third-world agricultural development, a good portion of it for biotechnology and the production of genetically modified seed. But increasingly the Gates Foundation has sought to provide support for local, sustainable agriculture. It is now encouraging indigenous farmers in Africa and funding a local crop-improvement center at the University of KwaZulu-Natal in South Africa.

The U.S. government, in response to lobbying efforts by groups like Bread for the World, has gotten the message. The George W. Bush administration agreed to spend a portion of U.S. aid on buying local crops and improving in-country infrastructure—a policy the Obama administration has continued. The aim is to promote local agriculture, save vast sums spent on long-distance shipping, maintain and improve biodiversity, conserve land, and slow population displacement.

Norman Borlaug's great project of helping poor nations feed themselves now requires methods different from those Borlaug himself introduced. And it requires good politics as much as it requires good agriculture.

| *"Despite rapid population growth, the prevalence of malnutrition did not worsen."*

Global Population Growth Will Not Cause More Hunger

Robert Paarlberg

In the early 1970s, the export prices of wheat and corn rose sharply on the global market, triggering declarations of a global food crisis. Recent increasing food prices have sparked similar concerns, focusing concern on food shortages, often in connection with population growth. In the viewpoint that follows, Robert Paarlberg argues that these warning cries are often deceptive. For example, the people who are experiencing the highest levels of food insecurity are not the people who are most effected by sudden global market price increases, Paarlberg contends. He traces the similarities between the 1970 crisis and current ones and finds that population increases are still being blamed for the shifting prices. Furthermore, he points out that food price increases tend to exacerbate unjust fears that the world is running out of everything. While he does not deny that aid is needed to assist farmers in regions where farmland is poor and farming

Robert Paarlberg, "The Real Food Crisis," *Chronicle of Higher Education*, vol. 54, June 27, 2008. Copyright © 2008 by Chronicle of Higher Education. Reproduced by permission of the author.

methods outdated, Paarlberg stands firm in his belief that food crises are local events, not global ones. Robert Paarlberg is a professor of political science at Wellesley College, an associate at the Weatherhead Center for International Affairs at Harvard University, and author of the book Starved for Science: How Biotechnology Is Being Kept Out of Africa.

As you read, consider the following questions:

1. According to Paarlberg, why are South Asia and Sub-Saharan Africa often immune to global food price fluctuations?

2. During what time period at the end of the twentieth century did poor countries experience declines in food security, as stated by the author?

3. How did the US aid programs and World Bank lending for agriculture change in the decades following the "bursting of the 1970s commodity-price bubble," according to Paarlberg?

Is the world really facing a food crisis? Export prices of basic food grains—corn, rice, and wheat—have certainly spiked upward this year [2008], indicating a scarcity of exportable supplies relative to commercial demand. Yet export prices on the world market are an imprecise measure of actual human hardship, since the world's poorest and most vulnerable citizens do not have regular access to world food markets. Instead those poor and hungry people, who primarily live in the countryside of sub-Saharan Africa and South Asia, tend to rely on local rather than global food systems, and many of those people remain malnourished even when international prices are low.

South Asia and Africa tend to import very little food. Only about 6 percent of South Asian grain is imported, and sub-Saharan Africa imports only about 10 percent of its total caloric consumption. And it is the more prosperous city dwellers who purchase what little is imported. So when import prices rise, urban consumers do feel a squeeze (particularly if fuel prices are also high), and they may even express their displeasure by taking to the streets. The results can threaten political stability and are easily captured by the international news media. Yet even when international prices are high, these urban dwellers are usually better fed than their fellow citizens in the countryside.

Local, Not Global

We might gain some insight into today's food economy from a comparable interlude that occurred roughly three decades ago. Between 1971 and 1974, the export price of wheat suddenly doubled, and the export price of corn increased by 60 percent. World reserve stocks of grain shrank by more than half. The price of soybeans rose so steeply in the United States that the federal government placed a momentary ban on exports. The United Nations Food and Agriculture Organization convened a food-crisis summit in Rome.

In that earlier case, international markets had indeed tightened, and the higher prices did lead to significant consumption cutbacks, but mostly by the well-to-do, who were then (and still are) the primary users of international markets. Because of higher corn prices, the United States reduced the feeding of grain to livestock by 25 percent, which led to higher meat prices and less meat consumption, but primarily among the well fed. In most poor countries, because supplies from the world market were a relatively unimportant part of consumption, higher world prices had little adverse impact. Data from the U.N. organization later revealed that, between 1971 and 1974 in most poor countries, the consumption of cereals actually increased on a per-capita basis. Over the 1970s as a whole, despite rapid population growth, the prevalence of malnutrition did not worsen in South Asia or sub-Saharan Africa, and in Latin America and developing East Asia hunger actually declined sharply.

Ironically, it was only when the so-called food crisis of the 1970s came to an end, during the slow-growth decade of the 1980s, that food circumstances in poor countries significantly worsened. In Latin America, even though world food prices were falling sharply, the number of hungry people increased from 46 million to more than 60 million. The reason was a regional "debt crisis" triggered by higher U.S. interest rates after 1979. The number of hungry people also increased sharply in Africa during the 1980s. The reason was faltering farm production, exacerbated in some regions by severe drought and civil conflict. The price for imported food was down, but hunger was up. Most real food crises are local rather than global.

Roots of Global Food Shortage Panics

There are some important similarities between the so-called world food crisis of the 1970s and the current situation. Then, just as now, oil prices were rising sharply. In fact, all commodity prices increased, just like today, creating an illusion that the world was running out of everything at the same time. Back in the 1970s, Lester R. Brown, president of the Earth Policy Institute, went on television to describe the apparent scarcities as the inevitable result of uncontrolled human population growth, just as he is doing again today.

It is no coincidence that monetary policies in the 1970s also bear a striking resemblance to the present day's. Then, as now, commodity-price inflation was being fueled by lax money policy. Back then it was Federal Reserve Chairman Arthur F. Burns loosening the money supply in order to get President Richard M. Nixon re-elected in 1972. Today it is Federal Reserve Chairman Ben S. Bernanke who has cut the federal funds rate seven times since September [2007] in an effort to save vulnerable financial institutions that made bad loans to subprime borrowers at the peak of the housing bubble. In the 1970s, just like today, loose monetary policies drove down the value of the dollar, which brought still higher prices for all commodities traded in dollars.

Just like today, export restrictions put in place in the 1970s helped exacerbate the illusion of a global shortage. In the 1970s, Europe imposed export taxes to stabilize the continent's food prices, a move that pushed prices on the world market still higher. Today it is a collection of rice-exporting countries in Asia—Vietnam, Cambodia, Indonesia, India, and China— that have blocked exports in the hope of stabilizing prices at home. That tactic has driven up international prices even though there is no global shortage (rice production in the past year actually rose faster than consumption). Fortunately, only about 7 percent of global rice demand is satisfied through these disrupted international markets.

Unlike in the 1970s, prices in animal-feed markets (and therefore in meat and dairy markets) are elevated in part because supplies of corn and soybeans have been diverted to the production of biofuels. Yet, although some critics blame government subsidies for that, today's outrageously high oil prices would be diverting significant amounts of corn into ethanol production with or without the government's support.

False Comfort

The most-worrisome comparison between the 1970s and today is possibly yet to come. If international food prices begin to fall back down in the next year or two—perhaps following a tightening of monetary policy, or a slowing of the world economy, or a bumper harvest this summer—there is a danger that international policy makers will decide the world's "food crisis" is over. If that happens, many of the critical new investments just now being made to boost food production in the developing world might be cut back, as they were in the

Rising Food Prices Are Not Linked to Population Increases

Certainly, grain and oilseed prices have doubled in two years—evidence, say the sceptics, that we are eating more than is sustainable and there is little room for additional consumption. But most of the increase in the cost of grain and oilseed is not pressures of population but from policy decisions. Rich countries are taking massive tracts of prime farmland out of food production. Increasing amounts of oilseeds are grown not for food, but to support a misplaced policy of so-called energy security for the US and a warm feeling of environmental goodness for the Europeans. . . . The impact of these policies has been to dramatically raise grain prices—the key food for most of the world's poor—by subsidizing some of the richest farmers on the planet.

Louise Staley,
Institute of Public Affairs Review, *March 2008.*

1980s. During the two decades that followed the bursting of the 1970s commodity-price bubble, the United States began to cut the share of its foreign aid that went toward agriculture from 25 percent of the total down to just 1 percent as of 2007. The share of total World Bank lending that went for agricultural development fell from 30 percent down to just 8 percent. In part as a consequence, agricultural development in the aid-dependent countries of Africa stagnated. Under a deceptive cover of much lower world food prices, hunger levels in rural Africa steadily increased. Between 1975 and 1995, the number of malnourished children in sub-Saharan Africa increased by 70 percent, mostly because farm production per capita was falling by 12 percent. By 2005, which was still a year of low international food prices, 23 out of 37 countries in sub-Saharan Africa were consuming less than their nutritional requirements, and one-third of all African citizens were malnourished.

Lack of Modern Farming Methods

The real food crisis in Africa today comes not from high prices on the world market but from low productivity on the local farm. Two-thirds of all Africans depend on farming for their income and their subsistence, yet because their farming techniques remain relatively unimproved by modern technology (most lack improved seeds, fertilizers, irrigation, electrical power, veterinary medicine, and modern transport), their crop yields are one-tenth as high as in the developed world, and only one-third as high as in the more successful developing countries of Asia.

It has been gratifying to see how this episode of high world food prices has brought renewed attention, especially from the World Bank, to the plight of poor farmers in the African countryside. This time around donor support must continue even after the deceptive price surge recedes.

| *"Continued population growth . . . is one of the surest ways to further job instability and depress wages."*

Continued Population Growth Will Harm Economies Worldwide

Deborah Rich and Jason Mark

Some experts see population growth as a necessary condition for the expansion and prosperity of an economy. Without enough workers and consumers, many contend, an economy will stagnate and decline. In the following viewpoint, however, Deborah Rich and Jason Mark argue that economies worldwide experience hardship in the form of declining wages, lifestyles, and natural resources as a result of ever-increasing populations. These problems, the authors maintain, could be mitigated if population growth slowed or declined because while fewer people would likely result in a shrinking of the gross domestic product (GDP), overall quality of life, employment rates, and wages would increase—all measures not considered in current GDP calculations. Growth and prosperity cannot be gauged by GDP alone, the authors state; thus, current concepts of these factors must be reformed to allow for population declines. Deborah Rich

Deborah Rich and Jason Mark, "Hold Steady," *Earth Island Journal*, vol. 24, no. 2, Summer 2009. Copyright © 2009 by Earth Island Journal. Reproduced by permission.

is a journalist who contributes regularly to the San Francisco Chronicle. *Jason Mark is the editor of* Earth Island Journal *and the coauthor of the books* Building the Green Economy: Success Stories from the Grassroots *and* Insurrection: Citizen Challenges to Corporate Power.

As you read, consider the following questions:

1. According to the *Economist* article cited by the authors, how did US economic performance compare to Japan's before and after correcting for population growth?

2. As stated by the authors, why will GDP declines that accompany population declines not increase "aggregate unemployment"?

3. What are the two ways in which a population can reach a "steady state," according to Rich and Mark?

It's highly unlikely that life as we know it—or want it—can continue for long unless we rein in population growth. Too many measures indicate that the great mass of us burning fossil fuels, gobbling up renewable resources, and generating toxic trash is overloading our life support ecosystems. In the central North Pacific Ocean gyre, swirling plastic fragments now outweigh plankton 46 to one. The concentration of CO_2 [carbon dioxide] in the atmosphere is far higher today than at any point in the past 650,000 years, and climbing. Nearly one in four mammals is threatened with extinction, as is one in three amphibians and a quarter of all conifers. In many parts of the world, including the High Plains of North America, human water use exceeds annual average water replenishment; the United Nations predicts that by 2025, 1.8 billion people will be living in countries or regions with absolute water scarcity. Unsustainable farming practices cause the destruction and abandonment of almost 30 million acres of arable land each year. The list runs far too long.

Meanwhile, our population continues to grow in leapfrog fashion. Despite declines over the last several decades in the annual global population growth rate and near zero population growth in several countries, the number of humans is still increasing by 1.18 percent per year. That sounds manageable—until we do the math. With more than 6.7 billion of us, even a growth rate of just over one percent translates into 80 million more of us annually, the equivalent of nearly two Sudans, or three and a half Taiwans. Each year, China must find room and resources for eight million more people even though its population is growing by only a little more than a half of one percent annually. The US, with a growth rate of nearly one percent per year, increases by more than 2.9 million people annually, the equivalent of almost four new San Franciscos.

Economic Growth and Population Growth

But dare we, as a matter of international or domestic policy, make an effort to reduce our population to a size that better fits our environment? Given that our economy is based on the idea of growth, wouldn't a decrease in human numbers lead to a fiscal catastrophe? After all, it's no coincidence that the last 200 years of historically unprecedented economic growth have been accompanied by an equally unprecedented increase in world population. During the 1800s and 1900s, up to half of world economic growth was likely due to population growth. As Georgetown University environmental historian John McNeill explains: "A big part of economic growth to date consists of population growth. More hands, more work, more things produced."

Global zero population growth might be an environmental imperative, but could it lead to an economic implosion?

The size of a nation's economy, usually summarized as its Gross Domestic Product (GDP), boils down to population multiplied by per capita income. Slow population growth, and economic growth will likely slow as well unless advances in productivity and spending increase at rates high enough to make up the difference. Maybe this is one reason why population policy, especially in the United States, remains a side issue. Our economic culture takes growth in consumer activity as both a given and a necessity. And if we assume away environmental limits, then each additional consumer brings additional consumer activity. "It's been said," Herman Daly, author of *Steady-State Economics* and former senior economist at the World Bank, reminded me this spring, "that the fox doesn't advocate birth control for the rabbit."

Could it be, then, that we can't afford to stop producing more consumers however much we fear the widening cracks in our ecosystems, lest we risk a shrinking economy accompanied by unemployment and economic turmoil? The answer, despite the hue and cry that usually accompanies each dip in GDP, is both yes and no: GDP likely will fall if we can slow and stop population growth. But the sky won't.

Per Capita GDP

On March 13, 2008, the *Economist* reported that America's economic performance in the five years leading up to 2007 was not necessarily better than Japan's, despite the fact that the GDP of the US was growing at 2.9 percent per year compared to Japan's GDP growth rate of 2.1 percent. More important than focusing on GDP, the *Economist* argued, was taking a look at per capita GDP, which corrects for population growth.

"GDP growth figures flatter America's relative performance because its population is rising much faster, by 1 percent a year, thanks to immigration and a higher birthrate. In contrast, the number of Japanese citizens has been shrinking since 2005. Once you take account of this, Japan's GDP per head increased at an annual rate of 2.1 percent in the five years to 2007, slightly faster than America's 1.9 percent and much better than Germany's 1.4 percent. In other words, contrary to the popular pessimism about Japan's economy, it has actually enjoyed the biggest gain in average income among the big three rich economies."

Sometimes, then, an increase in GDP says as much about how crowded things are getting as it does about fundamental economic strength. Conversely, a slowing or stopping of GDP growth caused by a reduction in population growth does not mean that our personal prospects have diminished. "Population decline does not imply any economic hardships," McNeill says. "Population decline would certainly slow the rate of economic growth, but it would not necessarily reduce per capita wealth or, indeed, per capita growth."

Nicholas Eberstadt, a political economist at the American Enterprise Institute, the influential conservative think tank, concurs. "I'm not convinced," Eberstadt says, "that population growth is a necessary condition for continuing or accelerating improvements in material well-being."

Let's be clear that we're talking about an orderly and relatively slow reduction in population, and not a chaotic plunge in our numbers as a result of war, disease, a breakdown in healthcare systems, or natural catastrophe. "The components really matter in this," says Eberstadt. "The way in which births and deaths are matched matters immensely."

Population Declines as Economically Beneficial

Ironically, the economic impact of any planned population decline would be dampened due to how numerous and technologically advanced we already are. We long ago grew plentiful enough and developed the transportation and communication systems necessary for the Smithian [after Scottish economist Adam Smith] specialization of labor that underlies modern economies. Few situations exist anymore where the marginal benefits gained from increasing national populations outweigh the marginal costs, especially when we count environmental costs.

"The advantages that may come with population growth have almost everywhere already been reaped," McNeill says. "China experienced rapid population growth in the 18th century and in most of the 20th century, which was, from the point of view of increasing the economic product and also the per capita economic product in China, probably a useful thing. Chinese agriculture is very labor intensive. If you don't have enough people, you cannot maintain the infrastructure of rice production: paddies, canals, etc. But once you have enough people to do that, then additional people are not helpful. They may be able to increase the total product, but they're likely to have a depressing impact on per capita economic product."

Daniel O'Neill of the Center for the Advancement of a Steady State Economy agrees: "At this point in history, having too many people, or too high a level of consumption, is much more likely to result in the end of economic progress, via ecological collapse, than having too few."

Neither does a decline in GDP caused by reduced population growth raise the specter of increased aggregate unemployment. An economic "slow-down" that results from slowing and eliminating population growth is distinctly different from that caused by a credit crunch or the messy bursting of a speculative bubble. While it's true there will be fewer mouths to pour breakfast cereal and soda into, there will also be fewer pairs of hands needing employment.

"When everybody is potentially a producer and a consumer, if you have one less producer in your society, you will also have one less consumer," says Peter Victor, an economist at York University in Toronto. "I don't see why that is bad for the economy. Production has gone down, but so has consumption."

A Steady State Economy Is Necessary

The Earth as a whole is approximately a 'steady state'. Neither the surface nor the mass of the earth is growing or shrinking; the inflow of energy to the Earth is equal to the outflow; and material imports from space are roughly equal to exports (both negligible).

In the last 60 years the global population has tripled and the amount of things our population has produced has increased by many times more, increasing our draw on natural capital, as well as on the earth's capacity to deal with the waste produced by all that we produce. . . .

But the facts are plain and incontestable: the biosphere that supports us is finite, non-growing, closed and constrained by the laws of thermodynamics. Any subsystem, such as the economy, must at some point cease growing and adapt itself to the dynamic equilibrium— the steady state—of the planet.

Herman E. Daly, Ecologist, April 2008.

Continued population growth, meanwhile, is one of the surest ways to further job instability and depress wages. In many poorer nations, sky-rocketing populations and entrenched unemployment are two sides of the same tarnished coin. "If the laboring class is having more children, then that means wages are going to have a harder time going up— you're increasing the supply or labor," Daly says.

Economic Growth and Quality of Life

Mistaking population growth for economic well-being has to do with the limitations of the measuring stick itself. GDP, it turns out, is an exceptionally crude way of calculating societal progress. As each additional million of us goes out and buys goods and services and, in so doing, grows the economy, we also take our toll on social and environmental resources—a toll that usually gets counted as economic growth in GDP calculations.

First developed in the early 1930s by an American economist named Simon Kuznets as a means of tracking the size of the economy month to month and year to year, GDP simply tallies a country's total legal monetary transactions. (In reality, it's not so simple: Inflation must be accounted for, and care taken not to double-count inputs on their way to becoming final products.) When the tally goes up, we talk of the economy growing and strengthening, and when it declines, we worry that the economy is contracting, shrinking, weakening.

All recorded monetary transactions contribute to the total size of the economy and therefore to the growth of GDP, but not all transactions are created equal. "One of the biggest problems with using GDP as an indicator of economic progress is that it does not differentiate between costs and benefits," O'Neill says. "In the US, for example, the costs of economic growth began to exceed the benefits sometime in the late 1970s. In other words, as the economy has grown through increasing population and per capita consumption, we have been spending more and more money to fix the problems caused by growth itself."

A sure way that I can contribute to the US GDP, for example, is by buying lots of highly processed foods from across the country, becoming obese, purchasing a bigger car, paying for an additional seat on plane trips, and visiting the doctor's office and drugstore more often. I'd certainly be generating lots of additional transactions, but my quality of life would have declined, and my demands on society and the environment would have increased. . . .

Similarly, the costs of mitigating the stress imposed by a ballooning population on roads, schools, parks, agricultural land, air and water quality, government services, and ecosystems add to the total pool of a country's economic transactions. But the greater pool and its rising GDP hardly signify that the average citizen is enjoying a higher quality of life. Stop population growth, however, and many quality of life indicators would improve even as GDP likely declined. . . .

Finding an Equilibrium

While reducing population growth in an orderly fashion promises more economic good than ill, it will bring about social and economic challenges that even proponents of shrinking the population do not dismiss lightly. Of particular concern are the challenges associated with reducing the number of working age people relative to retirees.

The trick is to hit the sweet spot of a generational equilibrium between births and deaths. A population can achieve a "steady state," neither growing nor shrinking, one of two ways: either match high rates of birth with high rates of death (lots of people born to live short lives) or match low death rates with low birthrates. With little to be gained and much to be lost by promoting a high death rate, our success in reducing and stopping global population growth hinges on our ability to reduce birthrates. Doing so will fundamentally change the demographics of many countries as the ratio of younger people to older people declines.

"One of the things we know about a steady state population is that it will probably be a grayer population than we have today," Eberstadt says. "That would change the tenor of society. There would be a smaller proportion of children than we have today. Under current arrangements, that might put a lot of stress on our healthcare and Social Security systems. But if we looked rather unflinchingly at the actuarial sustainability of those systems, we could fix all that stuff in the long term." . . .

Rethinking Current Ideas of Progress

Capping population growth and possible GDP will require a profound rethinking of our notions of progress and political clout. Historically, power and prestige—whether on the individual or societal levels—have been linked to size. Governments have balked at the idea of shrinking populations because declining numbers suggest a diminishment of economic force and military might. Many ordinary citizens worry that a smaller economy may lead to fewer opportunities for themselves and their children. The biggest challenge, then, is convincing people that growth for growth's sake simply can't keep working.

> *"Economists have tended to focus on* population *growth, ignoring the changing age distribution within populations as they grow. Yet these changes are arguably as important as population growth."*

Demographic Changes Impact Economies More than Does Population Growth

David E. Bloom, David Canning, and Jaypee Sevilla

Most discussions of population's impact on economies tend to focus on growth as the main factor informing change. In the viewpoint that follows, however, David E. Bloom, David Canning, and Jaypee Sevilla argue that demographic changes within a population are more substantial in their impact on an economy than growth alone. The authors outline the ways in which demographic transition is currently occurring in the developing world and offer an explanation as to why this transition is having a larger effect on the economies of these countries than increases in population alone. They maintain that with the neces-

David E. Bloom, David Canning, and Jaypee Sevilla, "Chapter One: The Debate Over the Effects of Population Growth on Economic Growth; Chapter Two: Demographic Transitions and the Democratic Dividend," *The Demographic Dividend: A New Perspective on the Economic Consequences of Population Change.* Santa Monica, CA: Rand, 2003. Copyright © year by Rand Corpration. All rights reserved. Reproduced by permission.

sary policies in place, this demographic transition can increase employment opportunities, yet it does have the potential to create political instability if appropriate regulations are lacking. David E. Bloom is the chair of the Department of Global Health and Population at Harvard University. David Canning is a professor of economics and international health at Harvard University. Jaypee Sevilla is a research associate at the Harvard School of Public Health.

As you read, consider the following questions:

1. According to the authors, when and why did the demographic transition in the developing world begin?

2. What is the impact, as stated by Bloom, Canning, and Sevilla, of declining fertility rates in the developing world?

3. What do the authors identify as the mechanisms of demographic transition, and how do they define them?

The relationship between population change and economic growth remains a subject of debate among economists and demographers. They continue to disagree about whether population growth (a) restricts, (b) promotes, or (c) is independent of economic growth. Proponents of each view can point to research evidence to support their cases.

The utility of this debate has been hampered by its almost exclusive focus on population *size* and *growth*. Little attention has been paid to a critical variable: the *age structure* of the population (that is, the way in which the population is distributed across different age groups) and how it changes when populations grow. . . .

Understanding the relationship between population change and economic growth has taken on immense significance in recent years because of demographic trends in the developing world. The world's developing countries—home to the vast majority of the world's population—are in varying stages of a demographic transition from high to low rates of mortality and fertility. This transition is producing a boom generation that is gradually working its way through nations' age structures. In conjunction with the right kinds of policies, this phenomenon creates opportunities for economic growth in developing countries. For this reason, policymakers should benefit from a clearer understanding of the relationship between economic development and the shifting age structure that results from the unfolding demographic transition. . . .

The Importance of Age Structure

Proponents of population pessimism, optimism, and neutralism can all fall back on theoretical models and more or less robust data to support their positions.

All of these theories, however, tend to ignore a critical dimension of population dynamics: populations' evolving *age structure*. Economists have tended to focus on population *growth*, ignoring the changing age distribution within populations as they grow. Yet these changes are arguably as important as population growth. Each age group in a population behaves differently, with distinct economic consequences: The young require intensive investment in health and education, prime-age adults supply labor and savings, and the aged require health care and retirement income. When the relative size of each of these groups in a population changes, so does the relative intensity of these economic behaviors. This matters significantly to a country's income growth prospects. Policymakers with a broad view of development and the complex relation between economic and human development must factor these effects of changing age structure into decisions about their countries' future.

This challenge is especially pressing in the developing world. In those countries whose mortality and fertility rates are beginning to fall (South Central Asia and much of sub-

Saharan Africa, for example), there is an opportunity for governments to capitalize on the consequent demographic transition, where the number of working-age adults grows large relative to the dependent population and potentially acts as a major economic spur. Conversely, if the appropriate policy environment is not in place, unemployment and instability may result, and health, education, and social welfare systems may undergo unbearable strain. Those developing countries whose transition is advanced, on the other hand (Southeast Asia and Latin America), need to look to the future, adopting policies to cope with an aging population and optimize the remaining years of low dependency ratios....

A Demographic Transition

In much of the developing world, a demographic transition is under way, accelerating with the declines in mortality that began near the end of World War II. Improvements in medicine and public health—for instance, the introduction of antibiotics such as penicillin; treatments for diseases such as tuberculosis and diarrhea; and the use of DDT [an insecticide], which helps control malaria—have contained or eradicated diseases that once killed millions of people. These advances were accompanied by improved sanitation, better nutrition, and the wider practice of healthier behaviors. All this gradually led to greater life expectancies, by as much as 20 years in some countries, and naturally to population growth, especially in developing regions. But despite higher life expectancies, these countries had populations that were, on average growing *younger*. This is because mortality declines were not evenly distributed across the population. Infectious diseases are particularly ruthless killers of the young, so their containment had the most powerful impact on the mortality of infants and children, which fell earlier and more quickly than mortality at other ages. The larger surviving youth cohorts served to drive down the average age of populations.

The mortality decline, which began the demographic transition, has been succeeded by equally dramatic reductions in fertility, especially in less-developed countries. Fertility decisions seem to respond strongly to changes in child mortality as parents realize that if fewer children are likely to die in childhood, they can give birth to fewer children to attain their desired number of offspring. This desire to rein in fertility is reflected in trends in the use of contraceptives. Worldwide, more than half of all couples now use contraception, compared with 10 percent in the 1960s. . . .

Other changes have reinforced the trend toward lower fertility, as it becomes advantageous to have smaller families. If children have a higher chance of survival and a long life expectancy, it is wise to invest intensively in them. A major form of investment is education—an investment that becomes more tempting when economic changes are likely to increase the potential returns on education. But this requires a long-term commitment. In a rural society, children typically start working on the land quite early and become economically productive at a young age. Educating children limits their productivity during childhood (they are at school rather than working). However, with increasing urbanization, children are less likely to be economically productive and the labor market will place a greater premium on skills, so education makes a greater difference to their future productivity. Thus urbanization raises the incentive of parents to educate their children while it reduces the opportunity cost of education in terms of forgone labor income. Because education is expensive, it becomes more likely that couples will choose to invest greater resources in fewer children. In addition, a greater emphasis on education will inevitably lead to more educated women. This reinforces the likelihood that families will become smaller: Women's time becomes more valuable and they are less likely to want to spend so much of their adult life bearing and raising children. For many reasons, then, smaller families make increasingly sound economic sense once the demographic transition gets under way.

The Lag Between Declines

The decline in mortality and the decline in fertility jointly form the demographic transition, but they are not synchronized. The lag between the two causes population growth, as fertility only begins to decline some time after mortality has dropped. This growth at the beginning of the demographic transition has preoccupied the prevailing views of population change and economic growth. However, the demographic transition also has a predictable impact on a country's age structure. At first, there is a cohort of children that includes many who would previously have suffered an early death. This baby-boom generation is unique: As fertility rates decline and families grow smaller, successive cohorts tend to be smaller. The result is a "bulge" in the age structure, a "demographic wave" that works its way through the population. . . .

[As a result], there are many young people, who need to be fed, clothed, housed, cared for medically, and educated. Then, they become adults who are more likely to spend only part of the income they generate on their own needs. The rest is used to provide for children or is saved, most often for retirement. Finally, there is a large cohort of elderly people, who work less—or not at all—and become "dependent" again. They either live off their own savings or are supported by their families or the state.

The effects of the modern demographic transition can be felt for several generations. An initial spurt of population growth occurs between the beginning of the mortality decline and the end of the fertility decline. But when the baby-boom generation itself reaches the prime reproductive years, it creates its own echo: a succeeding baby boom. Subsequent echo effects produce further spurts. In other words, even if total fertility rates have been reduced to replacement level (2.1 children per woman), the population will continue to grow until the members of the bulge generation and successive echo generations tend to have passed through their prime reproductive years. This process is called population momentum, and its effects will be felt for perhaps 50 to 100 years before the population age structure settles down. Because of the effect of population momentum alone, the population of developing countries as a whole is expected to increase by 40 percent between 1995 and 2100.

Changes Have Economic Results

While many economists have studied the effect of population growth on economic growth, far less attention has been paid to changes in the age structure brought about by the demographic transition. Combining the population growth rate and the growth rate of the *economically active* population captures the way that age structures change and delivers striking results. While population growth has a large and statistically significant negative effect on per capita income growth, this effect is counteracted by a statistically significant positive effect from growth in the share of the population that is economically active. While the age structure remains constant, therefore, the effect of population growth is neutral, but as the proportion of workers rises or falls, so do opportunities for economic growth. The demographic dividend, for example, was essential to East Asia's extraordinary economic achievements, accounting for as much as one-third of its "economic miracle". . . .

Without the right policy environment, countries will be too slow to adapt to their changing age structure and, at best, will miss an opportunity to secure high growth. At worst, where an increase in the working-age population is not matched by increased job opportunities, they will face costly penalties, such as rising unemployment and perhaps also higher crime rates and political instability. With no policies in place to provide for rising numbers of old people, many may face destitution in their final years.

In addition, the demographic dividend is time-limited. Many developed nations are facing the end of their demographic transition, and now must plan for their aging populations and a decline in their ratio of workers to dependents. . . . In all regions except Africa, the share of the population that is of working age will begin to decrease in the next 10–20 years.

Additionally, some are experiencing shrinking populations. Low fertility rates over an extended period of time, where replacement level is not reached, eventually lead to population decline. Italy's population, currently at 57 million, is projected to decline to 43 million by 2050. Japan's population is expected to decrease from 127 million to 109 million by 2050. The available labor force will decrease, and the elderly will increasingly make up a larger proportion of the population, bringing with it further social and economic challenges. Through the lens of demography at least, the next 50 years presents the developed world with significant challenges, at the same time as it offers the developing world a number of appealing opportunities.

The Effect of Labor Supply

The demographic dividend is delivered through a number of mechanisms. The most important are labor supply, savings, and human capital.

The demographic transition affects labor supply in two ways. First, there is an essentially mechanical effect, based on the regular and inevitable aging of the baby-boom generation. When this generation is between 15 and 64, it is more likely to be working, thus lowering the ratio of dependents to non-dependents. During the peak working years of 20 to 54, this effect is especially strong. The number of people who would

An Unprecedented Demographic Transition

The world is in the midst of a historically unprecedented demographic transition that is having—and will continue to have—profound effects on the size and age structure of its population. Before 1900, world population growth was slow, the age structure of the population was broadly constant, and relatively few people lived beyond age 65. This began to change during the first half of the twentieth century as rising life expectancy boosted population growth, although initially there was little change in the age structure of the population. The second half of the twentieth century saw the start of another phase in this transition. Fertility rates declined dramatically—by almost one-half—causing population growth to slow, the share of the young in the population to decline, and the share of the elderly to increase. The share of the working-age population, however, changed little.

These global developments mask considerable variation between countries and regions that are the result of very different fertility, mortality, and migration trends. For example, although fertility rates have fallen almost universally in recent decades, they remain much higher in developing than in advanced countries, where they are generally below the replacement rate.

Nicoletta Batini, Tim Callen, and Warwick McKibbin,
International Monetary Fund, January 2006.

like to work (labor supply) therefore gets bigger and, provided the labor market can absorb the larger numbers of workers, per capita production increases.

Second, women are more likely to enter the workforce as family size declines. This effect is magnified by the fact that, with adult women themselves more likely to have been brought up in small families, they are more likely to be educated. This increases their productivity in the labor market, leading toward a stronger workforce and smaller families.

Resulting Growth in Savings

The demographic transition also encourages the growth of savings, thus improving a country's prospects for investment and growth. Again, there is an accounting effect as well as a behavioral effect at work. The young and the old consume more than they produce, whereas working-age people tend to have a higher level of economic output and also a higher level of savings. Further, people tend to save more between the ages of 40 and 65, when they are less likely to be investing in their children and the need to prepare for their retirement is becoming more pressing. So when large numbers of baby boomers start hitting their 40s, national savings will tend to rise. Incentives to make certain choices can reinforce this tendency to save among the new young baby boomers. Improved health, and longevity, make saving easier and more attractive. A healthy population must plan far in advance if it is to maintain its standard of living through decades of retirement. Pensions are made even more important by smaller families and the mobility that urbanization brings. An extended family often takes care of its own elderly relatives. A nuclear family, with both parents working, is far less likely to do so, although the two-earner family's increased assets make it better able to provide care financially, if not physically. Additionally, private household savings can provide the capital accumulation needed to finance growth, as seen in East Asia. Further work is needed, however, to take account of the institutional features of pension systems when assessing the importance of the demographic transition to the determination of national savings.

A Mechanism of Demographic Transition

Finally, the demographic transition has significant effects on investments in human capital, effects which are the least tangible, but may be the most significant and far-reaching. The demographic transition begins with changes in mortality that result in a population that lives longer and stays healthier. A longer life expectancy causes fundamental changes in the way that people live. Attitudes about education, family, retirement, the role of women, and work all tend to shift. A society, especially if it is taking full advantage of the demographic dividend, is certain to experience deep-rooted changes in its culture, as its people become more valuable assets. Take education, for example: The positive correlation between education and earnings is well-known. In Latin America, for example, a worker with six years of education earns an average of 50 percent more than one who has no formal education. The premium increases to 120 percent for those with 12 years of education (i.e., those finishing secondary school), and exceeds 200 percent for those with 17 years of education (i.e., those completing tertiary education). As life expectancy increases, parents are likely to choose to educate their children to more advanced levels. Healthier children, in turn, tend to experience greater cognitive development per year of schooling than their less healthy counterparts. The parents also know that there is a good chance that each child will benefit from schooling investments over a long working life and, with fewer children, can devote more time and money to each child. The result of this educational investment is that the labor force as a whole becomes more productive, promoting higher wages and a better standard of living. Women and men therefore tend to enter the workforce later, partly because they are being educated for longer, but they are likely to be more productive once they start working.

Good Policy Is Necessary

All these mechanisms are heavily dependent on the policy environment. A growing number of adults will only be productive if there is sufficient flexibility in the labor market to allow its expansion, and if there are macroeconomic policies that permit and encourage investment. Similarly, people will only save if they have access to adequate saving mechanisms and have confidence in domestic financial markets. Finally, the demographic transition creates conditions where people will tend to invest in their own and their children's health and education, offering great economic benefits, especially in the modern world's increasingly sophisticated economies. But governments invariably play a vital role in creating an environment where high-quality health and education provision is possible—necessary steps to make the most of their country's demographic opportunities.

Periodical and Internet Sources Bibliography

The following articles have been selected to supplement the diverse views presented in this chapter.

Vanessa Baird	"The Missing Pieces," *New Internationalist*, January 2010.
Alastair Bonnett	"Green Agendas and Grey Dawns," *New Statesman*, March 9, 2009.
Current Events	"Going Hungry," January 12, 2009.
Economist	"The 9-Billion People Question," February 26, 2011.
Robert Engelman	"A Population Strategy for the Planet," *Bulletin of the Atomic Scientists*, November/December 2008.
Steve Forbes	"Humanity Deniers," *Forbes*, April 13, 2009.
Robert F. Harrington	"Unlimited Population Rise on Limited Planet Is Untenable," *CCPA Monitor*, June 2009.
David Pimentel et al.	"Will Limited Land, Water, and Energy Control Human Population Numbers in the Future?," *Human Ecology*, October 2010.
Jeffrey D. Sachs	"Transgressing Planetary Boundaries," *Scientific American*, December 2009.
Roger Thurow	"The Fertile Continent," *Foreign Affairs*, November/December 2010.
Peter Wehner	"Keeping Them Out, Letting Them In," *Commentary*, July/August 2008.

How Should Population Growth Be Addressed?

Chapter Preface

In a September/October 2009 article for the *Humanist*, Joni Baird, codirector of the Pro-Choice League, argues, "With nearly 79 million newcomers on our planet each year it would behoove us to apply a systems approach in order to curb overpopulation, which threatens our ecosystem and, consequently, humanity." She advocates rekindling reproductive rights initiatives that once espoused the morality of bringing fewer children into the world to alleviate problems of poverty and hunger. Today, however, Baird believes the argument for curbing population growth should emphasize environmental concerns, including climate change.

Pointing to the International Humanist Ethical Union (IHEU) as a model for this type of activism, Baird claims, "The IHEU, in working to build a world where each child born should have an environment in which it may grow to reach its full human potential and realizing the impossibility of this if present population trends continue, calls on international agencies, national governments, humanist organizations, and people of goodwill everywhere to cooperate in order to limit population growth." To achieve a unity of vision in which the fate of the planet is tied to reproductive rights, Baird believes—as does the IHEU—that birth control and safe abortions should be made available to women worldwide. By teaching women about family planning and their rights concerning reproduction and then connecting these issues to a moral obligation to preserve the environment, Baird hopes women's health will improve and pressures on the planet's resources and climate will ease.

The merits of Baird's argument have not gone unchallenged. In an August 2009 column for *Women in Action*, Betsy Harmann, a professor of development studies, and Elizabeth Barajas-Román, the associate director of the Population and

Development Program at Massachusetts's Hampshire College, claim that overpopulation is not the most significant contributor to climate change. They contend that focusing on population control shifts the burden of blame away from the true culprits—fossil-fuel-based economies and corporate pollution. In a world expected to see a population rise of about 3 billion people by 2050, Harmann and Barajas-Román insist that "investments in public transport rather than private cars, cluster housing rather than suburbia, green energy rather than fossil fuels and nuclear, would do a lot to help a more populated planet." Curbing population growth, in their view, would do little to teach people how to conserve energy, demand more-fuel-efficient technologies, and embrace environmentally friendly policies of all stripes.

The authors of the viewpoints presented in the following chapter debate these and other means of controlling population growth. Like Baird, some advocate that the environment should be protected by instituting policies ranging from contraception and family planning to immigration control. Others worry that such measures may be too harsh or impractical. At least one author asserts that curbing population growth in industrialized nations may create more problems than it solves. All of these experts, however, are conscious of the fact that the future looms as a time when more and more people will be competing for fewer and fewer resources.

"The United States has a financial and
moral obligation to ... global family
planning efforts [that] begins with ...
releasing UN [Population Fund]
funds."

The United States
Should Support the
UN Population Fund

Sneha Barot

*In the following viewpoint, Sneha Barot reports that the United
Nations Population Fund has helped curb population growth
and establish reproductive rights in the developing world. In
Barot's estimation, the distribution of contraceptives and the
educational tools to use them properly has benefited mothers and
children in developing countries by reducing mortality rates and
preventing the transmission of disease. According to Barot, contraception and family planning have also empowered women in
these nations and assisted in the reduction of poverty that at-
tends unchecked population growth. For these reasons, Barot
calls upon the United States to reaffirm its commitment to funding family planning programs in developing nations. Sneha*

Sneha Barot, "Back to Basics: The Rationale for Increased Funds for International Family Planning," *Guttmacher Policy Review*, vol. 11, no. 3, Summer 2008, pp. 13–18. Reproduced by permission.

Barot is a senior public policy associate at the Guttmacher Institute, an organization that promotes global health and reproductive rights worldwide.

As you read, consider the following questions:

1. What is the "global gag rule" and why is it problematic, according to Barot?

2. As the author reports, how much does the United States currently contribute to global population assistance programs?

3. According to a United Kingdom Parliament report of 2007, cited by Barot, what percentage of economic growth in developing countries can be attributed to lower fertility rates?

Contributions from the U.S. government to voluntary family planning activities in developing countries have generated considerable successes over the last four decades. Yet, the U.S. family planning and reproductive health program, administered primarily through the U.S. Agency for International Development (USAID), has encountered and continues to face many roadblocks to further progress, including policy impediments to sound programming imposed by the government itself. Such self-imposed setbacks include the "Mexico City" policy, also known as the global gag rule, which renders local organizations that engage in privately funded abortion-related activities consistent with their own country's laws ineligible for U.S. support for contraceptive services. Additional policy constraints involve withdrawal of U.S. assistance to the United Nations Population Fund (UNFPA) on the grounds that UNFPA's support of voluntary contraceptive services in China is somehow tantamount to support of coercive abortion. While these policy problems have caused serious injury and will require repair, an equally important challenge for

policymakers under a new presidential administration will be
to remedy the trend of chronic underfunding of international
family planning programs.

Contraception in the Developing World

Over the last 30 years, as women in the developing world increasingly have desired smaller families, contraceptive use has
risen and fertility rates have fallen. Still, demographic surveys
indicate that the actual family size in most developing countries remains greater than the desired family size. This gap between the real and the ideal persists even in Sub-Saharan Africa, which still retains a preference for larger families and has
the highest fertility rates in the world.

According to *Adding It Up*, a joint report from the Guttmacher Institute and UNFPA, a total of $7.1 billion (in 2003
dollars) is spent annually on family planning services in the
developing world. These funds—from both donor countries
and recipient developing countries themselves—support contraceptive care for 504 million women, helping them to avoid
187 million unintended pregnancies and 60 million unplanned
births. However, approximately 201 million women in developing countries desire to either delay or limit their births, but
do not have access to modern contraceptives; 64 million of
these women use traditional methods such as periodic absti-
nence and withdrawal, which have high failure rates. The report concludes that providing family planning services to all
of these women would prevent an additional 52 million unintended pregnancies and a wide range of deleterious outcomes
from those pregnancies.

Unlike the provision of some types of health care, such as
childhood immunizations, meeting the need for contraceptive
services is an ongoing imperative. The typical woman who
wants only two children (increasingly the worldwide norm)
will be pregnant, postpartum or seeking pregnancy for only a
few years of her life, but she will need to use contraceptives to

avoid additional pregnancies for some three decades. And the challenge only escalates as population growth itself increases, currently driven by 1.2 billion adolescents, the largest cohort of adolescents in history, who are approaching reproductive maturity and will need access to sexual and reproductive health information and services in the coming decades.

Benefits of Family Planning Programs

The United States has long been and remains the single largest donor country for population assistance in the world. Yet, over the last quarter-century, its position as global leader has been compromised by politically motivated programmatic restrictions imposed by successive presidential administrations, restrictions that have themselves been echoed in diminished levels of financial support. The bottom line is that at $461 million, current U.S. funding is only a small fraction of what it should be, according to the formulation derived at the 1994 International Conference on Population and Development in Cairo, Egypt.

As a result, international family planning advocates are embarking on an ambitious goal of more than doubling current funding to $1 billion. This amount—itself less than a third of the $3.2 billion it should be, according to updated estimates—is more than justified, because family planning is the key means to a broad range of critically important individual and societal development goals. First and foremost, of course, family planning enables women and couples to control their own reproductive destinies, an essential human freedom. At the same time, by preventing unintended, often high-risk pregnancies, family planning also saves women's lives and protects their health; improves infant survival rates and bolsters child health; reduces women's recourse to abortion and, especially, unsafe abortion; protects women and their partners against sexually transmitted infections (STIs), including HIV/AIDS; enhances women's status and promotes equality between men and women; fosters social and economic development and security at the family, community and country level; and helps safeguard the environment. These are compelling reasons, individually and collectively, to ramp up financial investment in international family planning programs.

Improving Maternal Health

A woman's ability to control the timing, spacing and total number of her children is critical to preserving her life and health. High-risk pregnancies—those that come too early, too often or too late in life—increase a woman's risk of pregnancy-related death. The impact of birth spacing alone on maternal mortality is dramatic. According to the World Bank, maternal mortality would drop by 25–35% if the unmet need for family planning were fulfilled for the estimated 137 million women in the developing world who are neither using a traditional nor a modern contraceptive method.

In addition, better timing and spacing of births could reduce the estimated 15 million women each year who face illness or disability from pregnancy-related complications, which in turn result in negative financial, social and health consequences for the women, their families and their communities. Insufficiently spaced pregnancies, along with inadequate prenatal, delivery and postpartum care, can jeopardize a woman's health on a temporary or permanent basis, through such conditions as anemia, obstetric fistula, hemorrhage, hypertension, infection and infertility.

Advancing Child Survival

Another high-impact public health benefit of family planning is in the area of child health and survival. USAID research shows that infants born closely together are at considerably higher risk of dying before their first birthday than are those with wider birth intervals. In fact, if women in developing countries could space their births three years apart, infant and under-five mortality rates would fall by 24% and 35%, respectively. The benefits of these longer birth intervals would also improve other health and nutrition indicators, such as the risk of stunting and underweight children.

The ability to delay births becomes even more important for the millions of young women who enter marriage at an early age. Adolescents are more vulnerable to complications of pregnancy and maternal death. Similarly, infants born to teen mothers, rather than women in their 20s and 30s, have double the risk of dying during their first year.

Reducing Women's Recourse to Abortion

The undeniable philosophical and political issues associated with abortion, at the individual and country level, are exacerbated in the context of the developing world, where abortions are largely illegal and unsafe. According to a 2007 study conducted by the World Health Organization (WHO) and the Guttmacher Institute, more than half (55%) of abortions in developing countries are unsafe; that proportion reaches as high as 95% in Africa and Latin America. Almost all abortion-related deaths occur in developing countries, accounting for 13% of overall maternal deaths worldwide.

Numerous studies have found that women in countries where abortion is illegal resort to abortion at similar rates as those living in countries where the procedure is legal. The most effective and efficient tool to prevent abortions is to prevent unintended pregnancies in the first place through the use of family planning. In the developing world, two-thirds of unintended pregnancies occur among women who are not using any method of contraception. In these countries, almost one-fifth of all pregnancies end in induced abortion. Satisfying the unmet need for contraception in these countries would further reduce women's recourse to abortion, beyond the substantial progress already made by current contraceptive use.

Preventing STIs, Including HIV/AIDS

Women who are sexually active are exposed to the dual risks of unintended pregnancy and STIs. The WHO cites unsafe sex as the second most important risk factor for disease, disability or death in the poorest countries. STIs, including HIV, are one of the leading causes of loss of healthy life among women. Women in their reproductive years are the fastest growing group of people contracting HIV, comprising more than half of those currently living with the virus.

Use of barrier methods of contraception—namely, the male and female condom—reduces the spread of STIs such as HIV from one partner to another—so-called horizontal transmission. Female condoms are particularly important, as they are the only available woman-controlled method that effectively protects against the sexual transmission of HIV. Additionally, by preventing pregnancies and births, all contraceptives play a significant role in prevention of "vertical transmission" of HIV. Although dedicated prevention of mother-to-child transmission (PMTCT) programs in developing countries substantially reduce the transmission of the virus to newborns through application of a short course of antiretroviral drugs, these interventions are not known, accessible or used by the vast majority of affected women in poor countries. Thus, it is extremely important to also supply contraceptives to women living with HIV who themselves desire to limit their childbearing. USAID has found that providing contraceptives to HIV-positive women who wish to avoid pregnancy could help prevent almost twice the number of child infections and almost four times the number of child deaths than stand-alone PMTCT programs.

Raising Women's Status

Beyond its medical benefits, investment in family planning generates powerful returns in other areas. The ability to control one's fertility is fundamental to raising women's status in society. Women who can decide when and how many children to have will be better positioned to negotiate decision-making in their households and to increase their life choices. Of particular importance is women's increased capacity to take advantage of educational and economic opportunities, and to enhance financial security at the household level. Women who cannot control the timing of their births are often doomed to poverty, as they struggle to raise more children than they would desire.

The impacts of fertility control and the education of young women are interrelated—both are necessary agents in improving women's status and contributing to a country's development. Education delays women's age at marriage and first birth, and contraceptive use decreases the likelihood that young women will drop out of school because of pregnancy. According to an analysis by the Millennium Project, among unmarried, sexually active, 15–17-year-old females, those enrolled in school were more likely than those not in school to use contraceptives. Another report by the POLICY Project estimated that 8–25% of young women in certain Sub-Saharan African countries drop out of school because of unwanted pregnancies. Not only does family planning help women avail themselves of schooling, but educated mothers and smaller families increase the likelihood that children, especially daughters, are also more educated.

Economic Growth and Social Stability

Family planning is essential to building socially and economically stronger families and fighting poverty. Families that can choose the number, timing and spacing of their children are better able to plan their lives, to save resources and to increase their household income. Families with more children have a higher risk of falling into poverty. Having fewer children allows parents to invest in their existing children and provide adequate nutrition, housing and education for the entire family. Moreover, women who control their fertility have more time for their own development and are more able to socially and politically participate in their communities.

The relationship between family planning and economic stability at the household level is also reflected at the community and national levels. Reduction of high fertility is a necessary although not sufficient factor in a country's path to economic development. According to a 2007 United Kingdom Parliament report on population, lower fertility accounts for 25–40% of economic growth in developing countries. Family planning decreases morbidity and mortality rates, and thereby produces a healthier and more productive workforce. Lower population growth reduces the burden on countries to make public expenditures for orphan care, family subsidies, food aid, health care, education and other social services.

The relationship between fertility and development has implications for a country's security as well. Expanding populations in poor regions can cause competition for limited resources, such as food, housing, schools and jobs, which in turn, can lead to societal instability. Failure to adopt family planning services has been identified as a key factor in the world's current food crisis. In the Philippines, for example, the government's refusal to support family planning services has been linked to a serious state of food insecurity. Explaining this phenomenon in a recent *Washington Post* article, a Filipino economics professor noted: "Even when there is widespread corruption, insurgent violence and other powerful reasons for poverty, the evidence from across Asia is that good population policy by itself contributes to significant poverty reduction."

Protecting the Environment

In the latter half of the 20th century, the earth's population more than doubled to six billion. It is expected to grow to more than nine billion by 2050, with almost all of the net increase occurring in developing countries that are least able and prepared to absorb this expansion. Unfortunately, millions of women in these countries currently wish to have smaller families—which would curb population growth—but do not have access to modern contraceptive methods that would help them achieve their childbearing goals.

There is a complex relationship among the effects of consumption and population growth on global environmental sustainability. One aspect of that relationship is that the rapid depletion of environmental resources in many poor countries is occurring to meet the needs of growing, migrating, urbanizing, and aging populations. These population pressures are straining the world's resources by diminishing safe water supplies, increasing carbon emissions, deforesting lands, and polluting the air and oceans. For example, the United Nations (UN) estimates that by 2025, more than three billion people will live in water-stressed countries, where basic water requirements for cooking, drinking and hygiene will be at risk. Climate change will contribute to less rainfall in regions such as North Africa, while demand for water in these areas will rise. Lack of adequate and safe water will endanger staple food production, exacerbate malnutrition and spread disease from lack of adequate sanitation.

The Need for US Support

At a recent conference of the UN Commission on Population and Development, UN Secretary-General Ban Ki-moon and UNFPA Executive Director Thoraya Ahmed Obaid singled out the downward trend in international funding for family planning as endangering the realization of the Millennium Development Goals, established in 2000 to set objectives for addressing poverty, health and women's empowerment in developing countries. A UN report released at the meeting noted that global funding for family planning services plummeted between 1995 and 2006. The Secretary-General warned

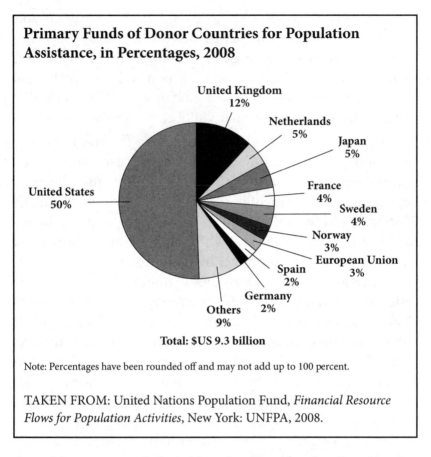

Primary Funds of Donor Countries for Population Assistance, in Percentages, 2008

United States 50%

United Kingdom 12%

Netherlands 5%

Japan 5%

France 4%

Sweden 4%

Norway 3%

European Union 3%

Spain 2%

Germany 2%

Others 9%

Total: $US 9.3 billion

Note: Percentages have been rounded off and may not add up to 100 percent.

TAKEN FROM: United Nations Population Fund, *Financial Resource Flows for Population Activities*, New York: UNFPA, 2008.

that this pattern of shrinking funding for family planning poses "serious implications for the ability of countries to address the unmet need for such services, and could undermine efforts to prevent unintended pregnancies and reduce maternal and infant mortality."

Against this backdrop, the United States has a financial and moral obligation to reduce the deficiencies in services, in funding, in policy formulation and in direction for global family planning efforts. Reasserting this leadership begins with overturning the global gag rule and releasing UNFPA funds. It continues with reprioritizing and reinvigorating financial assistance for international family planning activities—assistance that must be sustained over the long haul, since using family planning services is not a one-time event for individuals and couples, but a need that lasts throughout an individual's reproductive life, and will rise globally with increased population growth. Finally, U.S. leadership should serve as a call to action for all countries to step up and put family planning back on the agenda as an important foreign assistance and development issue. Millions of women and families in the developing world are depending on this leadership.

"The U.S. should not only continue to avoid funding the U.N. Population Fund, it should withdraw entirely from the organization."

The United States Should Not Support the UN Population Fund

Steven W. Mosher

Steven W. Mosher is the president of the Population Research Institute and the author of Population Control: Real Costs and Illusory Benefits. *In the following viewpoint, he objects to population control advocates blindly supporting the United Nations Population Fund (UNFPA) and its backing of what he sees as some reprehensible measures designed to limit population growth. Mosher asserts that China, for example, has carried out forced sterilizations to keep population growth in check, and he insists that the UNFPA has provided sanction and financial aid to China's program. Beyond such egregious examples, Mosher believes population growth programs have traditionally failed to*

Steven W. Mosher, "What Is Wrong with the UN Population Fund?," Huffington Post, January 1, 2009. Copyright © 2009 www.huffingtonpost.com. Reproduced by permission.

curb overpopulation and have only stripped poor people of their right to reproductive freedom. He hopes the United States will withdraw its support from the UNFPA.

As you read, consider the following questions:

1. In what countries does the UNFPA support coercive population control policies, as Mosher reports?

2. What kind of evidence does the author say the PRI has to support its claims that UNFPA is involved in coercive population control programs around the globe?

3. Why does Mosher believe that poor people—beyond those being abused by population control programs—are having their overall well-being compromised by UNFPA policies?

Why shouldn't the U.S. fund the population controllers at the United Nations, as *Huffington Post* columnist Cristina Page proposes [in a December 2, 2008, article]? The short answer is that the U.N. Population Fund (UNFPA) is implicated in some of the most coercive anti-people campaigns in the world today.

Started in 1969 following a massive lobbying effort by billionaire John D. Rockefeller III, the UNFPA claims to work to "reduce poverty and to ensure that every pregnancy is wanted, every birth is safe, every young person is free of HIV/AIDS, and every girl and woman is treated with dignity and respect." In fact, the UNFPA, like its founder, believes that the way to reduce poverty is to reduce the numbers of the poor through sterilization, contraception, and abortion campaigns.

Coercive Population Control

We know. We have conducted repeated investigations of UNFPA operations around the world. We have found that, despite its soothing rhetoric about improving "reproductive health," and "safe motherhood"—the UNFPA spends a huge chunk of its budget on soporific propaganda—the agency continues to be fixated on the numbers. We have documented its involvement in coercive population control policies in countries like China, Vietnam, Peru, and North Korea, as well as in refugee camps around the world.

Its intimate connection to China's brutal one-child policy merits special attention. For three long decades, the Chinese government has aborted and sterilized millions of women each year. For three long decades, the UNFPA has provided financial aid, ideological encouragement, and international sanction to these abuses through its offices in Beijing and around the Chinese countryside. This shameless pattern of complicity in some of the worst human rights abuses on the planet is the chief reason why the [George W.] Bush administration, for seven years running, has refused to fund the UN agency.

We at PRI [Population Research Institute] have hard evidence on the UNFPA's involvement in coercion—videotapes, cassette tapes, written and spoken testimony from dozens of witnesses. Our information was verified by the U.S. State Department, and is accessible on our web site, as well as in our new video series: Exposure: Investigative Realism from PRI. Even Secretary of State Colin Powell, who in the past has been friendly towards the UNFPA, declared the UNFPA ineligible for U.S. funding because of its complicity in forced abortion and forced sterilization.

Mindless Propaganda

Now, none of this matters to the radical base of the population control movement, which remains determined to shovel as many U.S. tax dollars into the UNFPA maw as possible. Cristina Page went so far as to call us lunatics for daring to challenge the UNFPA's programs:

Just when UNFPA was succeeding in proving to the Chinese the one-child policy was not only inhumane but also ineffective, PRI swooped in with its claims of complicity. Bush, eager to lock lips with his fanatical base, ignored the advice of his own state department, as well as many allied nations, and opted to go with the swirly eyed lunacy of the six staffers of PRI. At their request, Bush quickly froze all U.S. funds to UNFPA, which represented 12 percent of its budget.

Like other population control hardliners, Ms. Page does not attempt to refute our evidence. Instead, she mindlessly recites the UNFPA's party line. Does anyone really [think] that the UNFPA is "succeeding"—after three long decades—in bringing an end to a policy that the Chinese government proudly proclaims will persist until 2050? Her claim that Bush ignored the advice of his state department is likewise a fantasy. What Colin Powell, Bush's first Secretary of State, actually said was: "Stop the Funding."

Ms. Page has no real arguments to make against us, which is probably why she resorts to sandlot slurs. But we stand by our research and our findings. And we remain firmly convinced that the UN Population Fund serves no useful purpose, and should be abolished.

Controlling the Lives of the Poor

The population control programs of the past half-century, born in the dark fear of "the unchecked growth in human numbers," have been a quiet but profound disaster for the poor and marginalized half of humanity. Hundreds of millions of poor women (and men) have had their fundamental rights—i.e., to control their own reproductive systems and to determine the number and spacing of their children—grossly violated. An even larger number have had their overall well-being compromised as resources have been drained away from primary health care programs, with some succumbing to HIV/AIDS and other epidemics. While the cost of such programs

The Funding Flows Again

In its June 26, 2008 report to Congress, the U.S. Department of State again confirmed that China's Population and Family Planning Law and its implementation are coercive and that the UNFPA continues to provide support for and participate in the management of the program. As a result, for fiscal year 2008, the UNFPA was again denied U.S. funding.

However, starting with the fiscal year 2009 appropriations, U.S. tax dollars began flowing to the UNFPA, despite its continued support of China's coercive population control program.

Denial, evasion, and opportunistic arguments cannot change the truth. Coerced abortion and coerced sterilization are realities in China. The United States has an obligation to take a stand for basic human rights and should not contribute to this human tragedy in any way.

National Committee for a Human Life Amendment,
Fact Sheet, August 2010.

in terms of human lives and suffering has been all too real, the promised benefits have proven largely illusory. Is the U.S. more secure, the global environment better protected, and the world wealthier today because of population control programs? Are the poor better off? The evidence suggests not.

The idea of controlling human fertility "for the good of the state and its people," as Beijing is fond of saying, is a 20th century anachronism. It deserves to be as thoroughly discredited as Marxist-Leninism, and for the same reason: It is at heart a philosophy of state coercion. In its more extreme manifestations in China and elsewhere, it has given rise to terror campaigns. But even in its mildest guises, it encourages a technocratic paternalism that effectively subjugates individual and familial fertility desires to the wishes of the state.

The U.S. should not only continue to avoid funding the U.N. Population Fund, it should withdraw entirely from the organization. As far as the UNFPA itself, this creation of Rockefeller and his cronies should be shut down. Whatever legitimate health functions it performs can be transferred to the World Health Organization, UNICEF [United Nations Children's Fund], or other international organizations. Some small programs, like that instituted to address the problem of obstetric fistula, may be worth saving. Others are Potemkin [propagandist] facades erected to con critics and deceive women.

We—and the women of China, Vietnam, North Korea, etc.—are not fooled.

> *"In order to seriously address environ-
> mental problems ... we must stop U.S.
> population growth ... [and] therefore,
> we should limit immigration."*

Limiting Immigration to Control Population Growth Will Protect the Environment

Philip Cafaro and Winthrop Staples III

Philip Cafaro is an associate professor of philosophy at Colorado State University. Winthrop Staples III is an environmental biologist. In the following viewpoint, Cafaro and Staples argue that US population growth has a negative effect on the environment. To the authors, increased population will lead to more urban and suburban sprawl, more automobiles, and more consumption—all of which lead to increasing greenhouse gas emissions. Cafaro and Staples conclude that the way to curb population growth and thus improve the environment is to limit the number of immigrants allowed into the country. Though an unpopular notion, restricting immigration, the authors maintain, is one of the few ways America can make good on its commitment to a sustainable future.

Philip Cafaro and Winthrop Staples III, "The Environmental Argument for Reducing Immigration to the United States," *Center for Immigration Studies Backgrounder*, June 2009. Copyright © 2009 by Center for Immigration Studies. Reproduced by permission.

As you read, consider the following questions:

1. According to Cafaro and Staples, during what decade of the twentieth century did America see the largest population increase?

2. As the authors report, by how much did the nation's CO_2 emissions increase in the period 1990–2003?

3. What do Cafaro and Staples think the annual US immigration quota should be to provide the nation with a sustainable future?

The environmental argument for reducing immigration to the United States is relatively straightforward and is based on the following five premises:

1. Immigration levels are at a historic high and immigration is now the main driver of U.S. population growth.

2. Population growth contributes significantly to a host of environmental problems within our borders.

3. A growing population increases America's large environmental footprint beyond our borders and our disproportionate role in stressing global environmental systems.

4. In order to seriously address environmental problems at home and become good global environmental citizens, we must stop U.S. population growth.

5. We are morally obligated to address our environmental problems and become good global environmental citizens. Therefore, we should limit immigration to the United States to the extent needed to stop U.S. population growth.

Avoiding the Issue of Population Growth

This conclusion rests on a straightforward commitment to mainstream environmentalism, easily confirmed empirical premises, and logic. Despite this, it is not the consensus position among American environmentalists.

Some environmentalists support continued high levels of immigration, while most are uncomfortable with the topic and avoid discussing it. So strong is this aversion that groups such as the Sierra Club, which during the 1970s prominently featured strong commitments to U.S. population stabilization, have dropped domestic population growth as an issue. Several years ago, the group Zero Population Growth went so far as to change its name to Population Connection ("PC" for short).

In 2006, the United States passed the 300 million mark in population—that's 95 million more people than were here for the first Earth Day in 1970—with little comment from environmentalists. In 2007, as Congress debated the first major overhaul of immigration policy in nearly 20 years, leaders from the principal environmental organizations remained silent about proposals that could have added hundreds of millions more Americans during the 21st century.

Like immigration policy for the past 50 years, immigration policy for the next 50 looks likely to be set with no regard for its environmental consequences. We believe this is a bad thing. As committed environmentalists, we would like to see our government set immigration policy (and all government policy) within the context of a commitment to sustainability. We don't believe that the goals we share with our fellow environmentalists and with a large majority of our fellow citizens—clean air and clean water; livable, uncrowded cities; sharing the land with the full complement of its native flora and fauna—are compatible with continued population growth. It is time to rein in this growth—or forth-rightly renounce the hope of living sustainably here in the United States.

The Argument for Limiting Immigration

Our claim, then, is that "the environmental argument" is sound and that America should scale back immigration. Some readers will disagree. So let's look at the argument in more detail.

Immigration levels are at a historic high and immigration is now the main driver of U.S. population growth. Consider some demographic history. Between 1900 and 2000, the U.S. population almost quadrupled, from 76 million to 281 million people. The largest decadal population increase was also the most recent: a 32.7 million increase between 1990 and 2000. This population growth resulted from a mixture of natural increase and immigration, which has varied widely over the past century.

From 1880 to the mid-1920s, America experienced an immigration boom, "the Great Wave," during which immigration averaged 600,000 annually. U.S. population numbers grew rapidly in these years, due to a combination of high birth rates and high levels of immigration. For the next 40 years, from 1925 to 1965, the United States had a relatively restrictive immigration policy, which allowed 200,000 people into the country annually, on average. The U.S. population grew substantially during this time, too, from 115 million to 194 million, primarily due to high rates of natural increase. During the 1950s, for example, American women had an average of 3.5 children each, far above the 2.1 total fertility rate (TFR) necessary to maintain the population of a nation with modern health care and sanitation.

By the 1970s, American women were averaging fewer babies—in 1975 the TFR stood at a lowest-ever 1.7—and the United States was well-positioned to transition from a growing to a stable population. One study found that without post-1970 immigration, the U.S. population would have leveled off below 250 million in the first few decades of this century. It didn't happen, however, because in 1965 and several times thereafter, Congress greatly increased immigration levels. Between 1965 and 1990, immigration averaged one million people annually—*five times the average in the previous four decades.* Since 1990, immigration has increased even more, to approximately 1.5 million annually (one million legal and half a million illegal)—the highest rate in history.

Projected US Population (Millions)

Year	Zero Series	Middle Series	Highest Series
2000	**274**	**275**	**276**
2010	288	300	309
2020	302	325	347
2030	313	351	391
2040	321	377	443
2050	**328**	**404**	**498**
2060	335	432	558
2070	343	464	625
2080	354	498	697
2090	366	534	774
2100	**377**	**571**	**854**

TAKEN FROM: Frederick Hollmann, Tammany Mulder, and Jeffrey Kallan, "Methodology and Assumptions for the Population Projections of the United States: 1999 to 2100." Population Division Working Paper 38, table F, Washington, DC: US Census Bureau, 2000. Cited in Philip Cafaro and Winthrop Staples III, "The Environmental Argument for Reducing Immigration to the United States," *Center for Immigration Studies Backgrounder*, June 2009.

For these reasons, the United States population has continued to grow, resulting in a missed opportunity to get one key aspect of sustainability—human numbers—under control. Currently our population stands at over 306 million people, and it continues to grow rapidly.

Such is our demographic past; what of our demographic future? The Grand Council of the Iroquois famously looked "seven generations" out concerning the impacts of their decisions. Looking four generations into the future, in 2000 the U.S. Census Bureau released population projections.

Each of the three projections or "series" holds fertility rates steady, while varying immigration levels, so annual immigration rates make the main difference between them. Under the zero immigration projection, the U.S. population continues to grow throughout the 21st century, adding over 100 million people by 2100. Under the middle projection, with immigration a little less than one million annually, we instead add nearly 300 million people and almost double our population by 2100. And under the highest scenario, with over two million immigrants annually, our population nearly triples by 2100, adding almost 600 million more people by the end of the century. Obviously, according to the Census Bureau, immigration makes a *huge* difference to future U.S. population numbers. So our first premise is true.

Effect on the Environment

Population growth contributes significantly to a host of environmental problems within our borders. For example in the past two decades sprawl, defined as new development on the fringes of existing urban and suburban areas, has come to be recognized as an important environmental problem in the United States. Between 1982 and 2001, the United States converted 34 million acres of forest, cropland, and pasture to developed uses, an area the size of Illinois. The average annual rate of land conversion increased from 1.4 million acres to 2.2 million acres over this time, and continues on an upward trend. Sprawl is an environmental problem for lots of reasons, including increased energy consumption, water consumption, air pollution, and habitat loss for wildlife. Habitat loss is by far the number one cause of species endangerment in the United States; unsurprisingly, some of the worst sprawl centers (such as southern Florida and the Los Angeles basin) also contain large numbers of endangered species.

What causes sprawl? Transportation policies that favor building roads over mass transit appear to be important sprawl generators. So are zoning laws that encourage "leapfrog" developments far out into the country, and tax policies that allow builders to pass many of the costs of new development on to current taxpayers rather than new home buyers. Between 1970 and 1990, these and other factors caused Americans' *per capita* land use in the hundred largest metropolitan areas to increase 22.6 percent. In these same areas during this same period, however, the amount of developed land increased 51.5 percent.

What accounts for this discrepancy? The number one cause of sprawl, by far: population growth. New houses, new shopping centers, and new roads are being built for new residents. . . . In recent decades, cities and states with the highest population growth rates have also shown the most sprawl.

The most comprehensive study to date on the causes of sprawl in the United States analyzed several dozen possible factors. Grouping together all those factors that can increase per capita land use and comparing these with the single factor of more "capitas," it found that in America between 1982 and 1997, 52 percent of sprawl was attributable to population increase, while 48 percent was attributable to misguided policies that increased land use per person.

Some "smart growth" advocates resist the conclusion that population growth is an important sprawl factor, partly because they don't want to obscure the need for good planning and land use policies. They point out that several metropolitan areas that lost population in recent decades exhibited significant sprawl, including St. Louis, Detroit, and Pittsburgh. Of America's 100 largest metropolitan areas, 11 lost population between 1970 and 1990, yet they sprawled an average of 26 percent. This shows that poor land use planning and bad transportation, zoning, and tax policies are indeed important in generating sprawl.

On the other hand, cities with growing populations sprawled even more. Several states that managed to *decrease* their per capita land use during this period also sprawled, due to high rates of population growth. From 1982 to 1995, Nevada decreased its per capita land use 26 percent while sprawling 37 percent, due to a whopping 90 percent population increase. Arizona decreased per capita land use 13 percent while its population increased 58 percent, generating 40 percent sprawl. This shows that population growth also causes sprawl.

The bottom line is that if we want to stop sprawl we must change the transportation, tax, zoning, *and population* policies that encourage it. We will not stop sprawl if we simply accept as inevitable that factor—population increase—which the best research shows accounts for over half of the problem. Nor will we solve our other major domestic environmental problems. That is because our second premise also is true.

Growing Greenhouse Gas Emissions

A growing population increases America's large environmental footprint beyond our borders and our disproportionate role in stressing global environmental systems. Consider global warming. Nothing mortifies American environmentalists more than our country's failure to show leadership in dealing with this, the most important environmental challenge facing the world in the 21st century. As the world's largest economy and historically largest greenhouse gas emitter, the United States has a moral obligation to lead the world in meeting this challenge. A good start would be striving to stabilize greenhouse gas emissions at 1990 levels (the [1997] Kyoto protocol, rejected by the United States, calls for an initial reduction of 5 percent below 1990 levels). Meeting even this modest objective will prove difficult, however, if our population continues to grow.

Look at the numbers. The United States' CO_2 emissions increased 20.4 percent between 1990 and 2005, from 4,991 to

6,009 million metric tons. That means we would have to decrease our emissions by 20.4 percent per person to get back to 1990 levels, *at our current population*. But if we double our population, as we are on track to do in six or seven decades, we will have to decrease per capita emissions 58.5 percent in order to reduce CO_2 emissions to 1990 levels—almost three times as great a per capita reduction. Such reductions will be much more expensive and demand greater sacrifice from Americans. They are thus less likely to happen.

"Hold on a minute," critics may respond. "We can and should cut our carbon emissions 60 percent or even more. The technologies exist and America is wealthy enough to meet our moral obligation to address global warming. The problem, above all, is Americans' hoggish overconsumption."

We agree. Limiting consumption must play an important role in addressing global warming. American environmentalists should work to enact policies that reduce our fossil fuel consumption as much as possible. Such policies should include increased taxes on fossil fuels, redirecting transportation funding from highway construction to mass transit, heavy subsidies for wind and solar power, large increases in auto fuel standards, improved building codes that reduce the energy needed for heating and cooling, and more.

However, re-engineering the world's largest economy and changing the consumption patterns of hundreds of millions of people are immense undertakings that will be difficult, expensive and (we may assume) only partly successful. [Former vice president, now environmental crusader] Al Gore has stated that global warming is "the moral challenge of our time"; many of us agree with him. But if Americans are serious about doing our part to limit global warming, the "multiplier effect" of population growth is too important to ignore.

Again, look at the numbers. Between 1990 and 2003, U.S. *per capita* CO_2 emissions increased 3.2 percent, while *total* U.S. CO_2 emissions increased 20.2 percent. Why the discrepancy? During that same period, America's population increased 16.1 percent. More people drove more cars, built more houses, etc. Population growth greatly increased total emissions, and it is *total* emissions, not per capita emissions, that quantify our full contribution to global warming.

Before we go on, please note: we do not claim that by itself, halting U.S. population growth will solve sprawl, or meet our global warming responsibilities. On the contrary, Americans must reduce our per capita consumption of land and energy in order to meet these challenges. On the other hand, the evidence clearly shows that recent population growth has increased Americans' total land and energy consumption and made these problems even worse. Americans must address both overconsumption and overpopulation if we hope to create a sustainable society and contribute to a sustainable world.

Clearly premises two and three are true: U.S. population growth contributes seriously to both domestic and global environmental problems. Can we go further, and state that reining in population growth is essential to environmental success? Yes, we can.

Curbing Population Growth

In order to seriously address environmental problems at home and become good global environmental citizens, we must stop U.S. population growth. It is of course possible to spin out scenarios in which America's population doubles, triples, or quadruples, and yet we still manage, through miracles of technological creativity or ethical self-sacrifice, to become ecologically sustainable. Perhaps, as techie magazines like *Discover* and *Wired* periodically suggest, we may begin building farms in high rises and let the rest of the landscape return to nature. Perhaps Americans will start taking seriously Jesus' sayings about the unimportance of wealth and material possessions, and focus instead on what is really important in life ("for where your treasure is, there will your heart be also.")

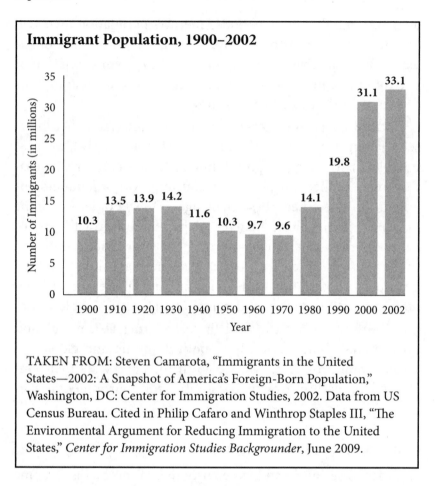

Immigrant Population, 1900–2002

TAKEN FROM: Steven Camarota, "Immigrants in the United States—2002: A Snapshot of America's Foreign-Born Population," Washington, DC: Center for Immigration Studies, 2002. Data from US Census Bureau. Cited in Philip Cafaro and Winthrop Staples III, "The Environmental Argument for Reducing Immigration to the United States," *Center for Immigration Studies Backgrounder*, June 2009.

Meanwhile, back in the real world, such scenarios are implausible. They are therefore morally suspect as a basis for action (or inaction). Given the difficulties of getting 300 million Americans to curb their consumption, there is no reason to think we will be able to achieve sustainability with two or three times as many Americans. . . .

Good Global Citizenship

We are morally obligated to address our environmental problems and become good global environmental citizens. We will not argue for this premise here, or provide a detailed statement of what it amounts to in practice. Environmentalism means many things to many people. Still, there are two general goals to which most environmentalists subscribe: (1) creating societies that leave sufficient natural resources for future human generations to live good lives; and (2) sharing the landscape generously with nonhuman beings. Let's call this "generous sustainability," to differentiate it from more selfish, economically-defined conceptions of sustainability.

We believe a moral commitment to "generous sustainability" captures the core of environmentalism. Numerous surveys in recent decades have shown that a large majority of Americans, from across the political spectrum, support these environmental goals. A commitment to generous sustainability is also explicitly endorsed by almost all philosophers writing about environmental ethics today. However, trying to convince skeptics of the truth of our fifth premise would require an article in itself (or perhaps a whole book!). Here, then, we take this moral commitment as a given, for the purpose of our argument.

To sum up, we claim that premises 1 through 5 of "the environmental argument for reducing immigration" are true—or at least that any serious environmentalist needs to treat them as true. But our conclusion necessarily follows from them. Therefore, our conclusion is also true: *we should limit immigration into the United States to the extent needed to stop U.S. population growth.*

A Proposed Policy to Reduce Immigration

We propose, then, that the United States reduce immigration by taking the following measures:

- Cut legal immigration from one million to 200,000 per year (the level allowed during the middle of the last century).

- Reduce illegal immigration by strictly enforcing sanctions against employers who hire illegal workers (it is

143

fruitless to try to lower legal immigration levels while ignoring or condoning illegal immigration).

- Rework trade agreements, and increase and better target development aid, to help people live better lives in their own countries.

Such a policy would allow some of the benefits of immigration to continue (providing asylum for political refugees, allowing small influxes of workers with special skills, etc.) while helping the United States move toward population stabilization. Because our current TFR of 2.05 is right around "replacement rate" (2.1) and because reducing immigration would likely help drive our TFR even lower, such stabilization is no wild eco-fantasy. The United States is nearly there, if we are willing to limit immigration (this also holds true for other developed nations, whose TFRs tend to be even lower than the United States').

This proposal is solidly within the mainstream of the best thinking on sustainability. As the President's Council on Sustainable Development put it in 1996: "Managing population growth, resources, and wastes is essential to ensuring that the total impact of these factors is within the bounds of sustainability. Stabilizing the population without changing consumption and waste production patterns would not be enough, but it would make an immensely challenging task more manageable. In the United States, each is necessary; neither alone is sufficient." One of the Council's 10 major suggestions for creating a sustainable society was: "Move toward stabilization of U.S. population."

Many readers will instinctively recoil from our proposal. But we contend that paeans to sustainability, or talk of non-human beings having an intrinsic value that we need to respect, or reminders that God calls us to be good stewards of His creation, or earnest expressions of our strong environmental feelings, are all mere cant, when coupled with a blithe acceptance of the doubling or tripling of America's human population.

> *"Focusing on immigration ... mistakenly links the trends of population and ecological harm, and so misdiagnoses the root causes of the current environmental crisis."*

Limiting Immigration to Control Population Growth Will Not Protect the Environment

Ian Angus and Simon Butler

In the viewpoint that follows, Ian Angus and Simon Butler insist that immigrants should not be blamed for increasing environmental dangers. For example, the authors refute arguments that developed nations should limit immigration to keep populations under control and thus stabilize greenhouse gas emissions. As Angus and Butler assert, the true culprits of greenhouse gas emissions are industries, not individuals. Blaming immigrants for environmental degradation supposedly brought on by overpopulation is simply a form of xenophobic fear mongering, the authors contend. Angus and Butler also worry that the anti-immigrant attitude is becoming so pervasive in the environmen-

tal movement that legitimate activists are adopting this view and damaging the integrity of the environmental cause. Ian Angus and Simon Butler are the coauthors of the book Too Many People? Population, Immigration, and the Environmental Crisis. *Angus is editor of the environmental website* Climate and Capitalism; *Butler is a member of Australia's Socialist Alliance and coeditor of* Green Left Weekly, *an Australian socialist newspaper.*

As you read, consider the following questions:

1. According to Angus and Butler, what has the "environmental" anti-immigration argument been in the past?

2. Why won't limiting immigration have a significant effect on CO_2 emissions in the United States, in the authors' opinion?

3. According to the Climate Justice and Migration Working Group, as cited by Angus and Butler, how many people worldwide have already been displaced by environmental change?

Immigrants to the developed world have frequently been blamed for unemployment, crime and other social ills. Attempts to reduce or block immigration have been justified as necessary measures to protect "our way of life" from alien influences.

Today, some environmentalists go farther, arguing that sharp cuts in immigration are needed to reduce greenhouse gas emissions and slow climate change. However sincere and well-meaning such activists may be, their arguments are wrong and dangerous, and should be rejected by the climate emergency movement.

Traditional Opposing Argument

"Environmental" arguments for reducing immigration aren't new. In a 1974 article, "Lifeboat Ethics: The Case Against

Helping the Poor," US biologist Garrett Hardin argued that "a nation's land has a limited capacity to support a population and as the current energy crisis has shown us, in some ways we have already exceeded the carrying capacity of our land." Immigration, he said, was "speeding up the destruction of the environment of the rich countries."

Elsewhere he wrote: "Overpopulation can be avoided only if borders are secure; otherwise poor and overpopulated nations will export their excess to richer and less populated nations."

Hardin's ideas have been very influential in the development of the right-wing, anti-immigration movement in the US and elsewhere. In 1979, he helped to found the Federation for American Immigration Reform (FAIR), an anti-immigrant lobbying group that has been named a "hate organization" by the Southern Poverty Law Center. In addition to the usual array of anti-immigrant arguments FAIR has made a particular point of linking concerns about the environment with opposition to immigration.

Virginia Abernethy, a Hardin collaborator who calls herself an "ethnic separatist," argues that the ability to migrate to rich countries gives people in poor countries an incentive to have bigger families: "The U.S. would help, not harm, by encouraging an appreciation of limits sooner rather than later. A relatively-closed U.S. border would create most vividly an image of limits and be an incentive to restrict family size."

A New Twist

In the past, the "environmental" anti-immigration argument was: *immigrants should be kept out because their way of life is a threat to our environment.* That argument is still made by anti-immigrant groups and some conservationists.

Even the highly respected U.S. environmentalist Bill Mc-Kibben has written that, "the immigration-limiters . . . have a reasonable point," because "If you're worried about shredding the global environment, the prospect of twice as many world-champion super-consumer Americans has got to worry you."

Noted environmentalist and journalist Tim Flannery made a similar argument during a debate on immigration policy broadcast by the Australian Broadcasting Corporation in September 2009:

> "Growing Australia's population has a much greater impact than growing the population of a poor country. We are the heaviest carbon users in the world, about 23 tonnes per capita, so people that come to this country from anywhere on the planet will result almost certainly in an increase carbon emissions. . . ."

As these examples show, "green" arguments against immigration are no longer the exclusive property of anti-immigrant bigots. They are increasingly heard within the climate movement, and so require strong answers from climate activists.

Ignoring the Real Culprits

The view that stopping immigration to wealthy countries is a good way to fight global warming rests on the simplistic idea that because immigrants come from countries with low per capita emissions to countries with high per capita emissions they supposedly increase total emissions simply by moving.

This argument is false on its face.

To calculate "per capita emissions," we simply divide a country's total greenhouse gas emissions by its total population. This provides a useful baseline for comparing countries of different sizes—but it tells us nothing at all about the emissions that can actually be attributed to individuals.

In fact, most emissions are caused by industrial and other processes over which individuals have no control.

In Canada, for example, no change in the number of immigrants will have any effect on the oil extraction industry at the Alberta Tar Sands, described by George Monbiot as "the world's biggest single industrial source of carbon emissions."

Reducing immigration to the United States will have no effect whatsoever on the massive military spending—up 50% in the past decade—which ensures that the Pentagon is the world's biggest consumer of oil. To put that in context: a study published in March 2008 found that the CO_2 emissions caused directly by the Iraq war until then were equivalent to putting 25 million more cars on the road in the U.S.

Closing Australia's borders would have had no effect on the climate denial policies of the previous Liberal Party government, or on the current Labor government's determination to continue Australia's role as "the world's largest 'coal mule.'"

As US immigrant rights campaigner Patricia Huang has pointed out, "the relationship between population growth and environmental destruction is shaped by how we use our resources, not by the number of people who use them."

Labeling migrants as a climate change problem is not only unjust, but it obscures the real challenges the climate movement faces. The decisive question we must address is who makes decisions about resource use in society. In capitalist society, the big financial institutions, multinational corporations and fossil-fuel companies wield this power with devastating results for the planet's ecosystems—and governments do their bidding.

Recently, as concern about greenhouse gas emissions and global warming increased, the anti-immigrant argument has taken on a new form. Now the argument is: *immigrants should be kept out because our way of life is a threat to the world's environment.*

That's the argument made in a recent briefing from the US Centre for Immigration Studies [CIS], a "think tank" founded by FAIR: it says that immigration worsens CO_2 emissions "because it transfers population from lower-polluting parts of the world to the United States, which is a higher polluting country." CIS calculated that the "average immigrant" to the US contributed four times more CO_2 than in their country of origin.

Otis Graham, a founder of FAIR, made the same argument in his 2004 book *Unguarded Gates*:

> "Most immigrants ... move from poor societies to richer ones, intending to do what they almost always succeed in doing, take on a higher standard of living that carries a larger ecological footprint. This being the case, the logic of the relationship is straightforward. Population growth in both poor and wealthy societies, but especially in the latter, intensifies environmental problems. Where immigration shifts population numbers to wealthier societies, it does not leave global environmental damage the same, but intensifies global as well as local environmental degradation."

A recent FAIR report claims that increased population is the primary cause of the huge increase in U.S. greenhouse gas emissions between 1973 and 2007—and that the population increase was caused by immigration. "The United States will not be able to achieve any meaningful reductions in CO_2 emissions without serious economic and social consequences for American citizens unless immigration is sharply curtailed."

The racist British National Party [BNP], which likes to call itself the "true green party" because it opposes immigration, also uses this argument. BNP leader Nick Griffin recently told the European parliament that climate change isn't real—but that hasn't stopped him saying immigrants will make it worse. He told author Steven Faris that by accepting immigrants from the third world, "We're massively increasing their impact of carbon release into the world's atmosphere. There's no doubt about it, the western way of life is not sustainable. So what on Earth is the point of turning more people into westerners?"

(It is significant that none of these supposed defenders of the environment take their argument to its logical conclusion: if immigration to the North is bad for the climate then emigration to poor countries with low emissions must be good and should be encouraged.)

Scapegoating Immigrants

The overpopulation and "let them stay home" arguments suggest that climate change and global poverty are insulated issues that exist within territorial borders. [Anti-immigration] proponents claim that sealing our borders will help our country solve its own environmental problems, and we should leave other countries to contend with theirs. This is a dangerous fallacy because . . . it distracts from the bigger issue. Climate change affects all countries indiscriminate of high and low emitters.

It's unjust to scapegoat immigrants for the environmental challenges we ourselves created and then prescribe anti-immigrant policy as a solution. We should instead support global solutions: financing more low-carbon energy projects in developing countries; attacking the real causes of climate change; and helping the United States become a leader in the fight against it.

Jorge Madrid, Center for American Progress, October 2010.

Disguised Fear Mongering

For anti-immigration bigots, concern for the environment is just a ploy—they'll say anything to justify keeping immigrants out. It's an example of what author and feminist activist Betsy Hartmann has called "the greening of hate—blaming environmental degradation on poor populations of color."

But it is particularly disturbing to witness the promotion of similar arguments in the mainstream media, and by environmental activists whose political views are otherwise hostile to those of FAIR and the BNP.

For example, Ross Gittins, economics editor of the *Sydney Morning Herald*, said in 2008 that cutting Australia's immigration was "one of the quickest and easiest ways to reduce the growth in our emissions" because "it's a safe bet they'd be emitting more in prosperous Australia than they were before."

Australian renewable energy expert Mark Diesendorf has urged the Australian Greens to call for immigration restrictions because Australia is such a big polluter. "Australia is world's biggest per capita emitter of greenhouse gases. So every additional Australian has a bigger impact than anywhere else."

Focusing on immigration diverts attention from the real social and economic causes of global warming, and makes it more difficult to solve them. This approach mistakenly links the trends of population and ecological harm, and so misdiagnoses the root causes of the current environmental crisis. It leaves social change out of the equation or consigns it to the far future. It downplays or ignores the fact that immigration would have a very different impact in the zero-emissions economy we need to fight for.

Undermining Legitimate Activism

As we've seen, the argument that reducing immigration will protect the environment originated with right-wing, anti-immigrant bigots. Our major concern, however, is that virtually identical arguments have been adopted by progressive activists and writers who are sincerely concerned about global warming.

Despite their sincerity, their arguments betray regrettable pessimism about our common ability to build a climate emergency movement that is powerful enough to win the anti-emissions fight. As Larry Lohmann of Cornerhouse writes, the anti-immigration argument "relies on the premise that changing Northern lifestyles is a lower priority, or less achievable, than preventing others from sharing them."

In fact, including "close the borders" as an anti-emissions demand tends to make their pessimistic outlook self-confirming, by making it more difficult to build a mass movement. Not only does targeting immigration divert attention from the social causes of global warming, but it divides us from our allies, while strengthening our enemies.

Sadly, some groups that favor immigration control seem oblivious to the danger of lending credibility to bigots and racists who view immigrants as a threat to "our" way of life.

For example, last year the Australian Conservation Foundation praised Labor MP [member of Parliament] Kelvin Thompson, and Sustainable Population Australia named him to its "Population Role of Honour" when he called for immigration cuts to deal with climate change. Both ignored the fact that just 10 days earlier Thomson had revealed his real motives by calling for immigration cuts "to minimize the risk that people who do not respect Australia's laws and legal system will enter this country."

The anti-immigration response to climate change raises a huge wall between the climate movement and the most oppressed working people in the imperialist countries. How can we possibly win migrants and refugees to the climate movement while simultaneously accusing them of responsibility for rising emissions and asking the government to bar them and their families from entering the country?

What's more, it undermines efforts to work with the growing and important climate justice movement in the Third World, where global warming is now producing its first and most devastating effects. How can we expect to be taken seriously as allies, if we tell those movements that migrants are not welcome in our countries?

The Climate Justice and Migration Working Group, an international coalition of human rights and immigrant rights groups, estimates that between 25 and 50 million people have already been displaced by environmental change, and that could rise to 150 million by 2050. It calls for recognition of the right of human mobility across borders as an essential response to the climate change threat.

The climate justice movement in the rich countries has a particular responsibility to support this demand—but blaming immigrants in general for global warming will make it more difficult to win public support for climate refugees.

Despite the good intentions of its green advocates, support for immigration controls strengthens the most regressive forces in our societies and weakens our ability to stop climate change.

It gives conservative governments and reactionary politicians an easy-out, allowing them to pose as friends of the environment by restricting immigration, while doing nothing to reduce real emissions.

It hands a weapon to climate change deniers, allowing them to portray the climate movement as hostile to the legitimate aspirations of the poorest and most oppressed people in the world.

People are not pollution. Inserting immigration into the climate change debate divides the environmental movement along race, class and gender lines, at a time when the broadest possible unity is essential. It is a dangerous diversion from the real issues, one the movement cannot afford and should not support.

Periodical and Internet Sources Bibliography

The following articles have been selected to supplement the diverse views presented in this chapter.

Asoka Bandarage	"Control Cash Not People," *Ecologist*, October 2008.
John Bongaarts and Steven W. Sinding	"A Response to Critics of Family Planning Programs," *International Perspectives on Sexual and Reproductive Health*, March 2009.
Paul Collins	"The Morality of Population Control," *Eureka Street*, December 18, 2009.
Matthew Connolly	"Controlling Passions," *Wilson Quarterly*, Summer 2008.
Scott Connolly, Katie Elmore, and William Ryerson	"U.S. Attitudes on Population," *World Watch*, September/October 2008.
Roy Jacobstein et al.	"Fragile, Threatened, and Still Urgently Needed: Family Planning Programs in Sub-Saharan Africa," *Studies in Family Planning*, June 2009.
Lawrence M. Krauss	"How Women Can Save the Planet," *Scientific American*, November 2009.
Kari Lydersen	"Border War," *Earth Island Journal*, Summer 2009.
Gar Smith	"Planet Girth," *Earth Island Journal*, Summer 2009.
Scott Victor Valentine	"Disarming the Population Bomb," *International Journal of Sustainable Development and World Ecology*, April 2010.

 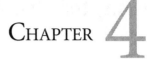

CHAPTER 4

What Will Be the Impact of Global Demographic Shifts?

Chapter Preface

Improved health care and decreasing birthrates around the globe are leading population experts to conclude that many countries—including China, India, and much of the Western world—will experience unusual shifts in demographic patterns over the next four decades. Namely, many nations will face populations composed of more old people and fewer young workers. These demographic realities are of great concern to bustling economies. China, for example, is rethinking its one-child-per-family policy because there may be too few workers to keep up its dramatic economic growth rate. Writing for *Forbes* in July 2009, former coeditor Paul Maidment claims, "Sometime in the next decade . . . China's working population will begin to grow more slowly than its total population" and "by 2050, China's seniors alone will likely constitute a larger nation than all Americans today."

Such snapshots of the future frighten policy makers across the globe. Shrinking workforces mean slower economic growth and fewer tax revenues. Aging populations translate to higher health care costs. Together, the two trends suggest budgetary shortfalls and inadequate welfare and medical coverage. In the United States, the Social Security Administration (SSA) predicts that the Social Security system will be bankrupt by 2040. The SSA suggests that delaying retirement and reforming pension benefits (to compel individuals to save more) are worthwhile proposals if the government cannot supply missing retirement funding from some other source.

Nicholas Eberstadt of the American Enterprise Institute, however, argues that the United States might be spared some of the trials that will surely impact the rest of the world's economic superpowers. In a November/December 2010 *Foreign Affairs* article, he claims that the US Census Bureau is predicting a growth in population over the next two decades. "Unlike all other affluent countries, the United States can expect a growing pool of working-age people," Eberstadt writes. A relatively high fertility rate and increasing immigration will provide the needed workforce and slow the statistical aging process. He maintains that "both factors would keep the nation growing and relatively young, shaping a distinctly more auspicious outlook for economic growth in the United States than exists for Japan or western Europe." Eberstadt is still cautious in his forecast, however. Although he credits the flow of immigrants for keeping America young, he points out that growing resistance to lax immigration policies and the fight for more stringent border controls could end the benefits of this demographic shift.

In the following chapter, other experts examine the social and economic impact of demographic changes taking place in the world. For instance, while industrial nations fret over the loss of youthful populations, Neil Howe and Richard Jackson warn that growing numbers of young people in developing countries may be a dangerous trend as more disempowered youth may turn to violence and political or religious extremism. Other authors in the chapter warn that shifts in demographics may lead to more pollution and a struggle for resources. Such assessments highlight the notion that population growth may not be as important a concern in the future than the movements of populations spurred by economic changes and social upheaval.

> "Dramatic demographic trends in developing nations . . . will give rise to dangerous new security threats."

Current Demographic Trends Threaten Global Security

Neil Howe and Richard Jackson

Neil Howe and Richard Jackson are, respectively, a senior associate and a senior fellow at the Center for Strategic and International Studies. They are coauthors of The Graying of the Great Powers: Demography and Geopolitics in the 21st Century. *In the viewpoint that follows, Howe and Jackson argue that while developed nations are witnessing fewer births and a rise in aging populations, many developing countries are still experiencing high growth rates within younger populations. To the authors, this is a concern because they maintain that violence is more likely to occur in countries with a large proportion of young males with limited opportunities. Therefore, Howe and Jackson caution that the developed world must closely monitor their "youthful" neighbors to guard against political instability, religious extremism, and the overthrow of democratic order that could affect global security.*

Neil Howe and Richard Jackson, "Battle of the (Youth) Bulge," *National Interest*, no. 96, July/August 2008, pp. 33–41.

As you read, consider the following questions:

1. What is the "demographic peace" thesis, as Howe and Jackson explain it?

2. Why do the authors believe developed nations may not be immune to instability even if their populations are aging?

3. Why do Howe and Jackson maintain that religious extremism will likely remain a threat even in countries that reduce poverty, increase access to education, and integrate their economies into the global marketplace?

Over the next few decades, the developed countries will age and weaken. Meanwhile, dramatic demographic trends in developing nations—from resurgent youth booms in the Muslim world to premature aging in China and population implosion in Russia—will give rise to dangerous new security threats. Some argue that global demographic trends are progressively pushing the world toward greater peace and prosperity. They are wrong. The risks of both chaotic state collapse and neoauthoritarian reaction are rising.

The Impact of Graying Populations

Everyone knows that the developed world is aging rapidly. Graying workforces will become less flexible, less mobile and less innovative; rates of savings and investment will decline; current-account balances will turn negative and foreign indebtedness will grow. Rising pension and health-care costs will place intense pressure on government budgets, crowding out spending on defense and international affairs; militaries will face growing manpower shortages.

Although it is less widely appreciated, the *developing world* is also aging. Like the developed world before it, the developing world is now in the midst of what demographers call the "demographic transition"—the shift from high mortality and high fertility to low mortality and low fertility that all societies undergo in the course of development. Since 1970, the average fertility rate in the developing world has fallen from 5.1 to 2.9. Meanwhile, the median age of the developing world has risen from 20 in 1970 to 26 in 2005. It is projected to keep rising to 31 in 2030 and 35 in 2050—at which point the typical developing country will be about as old as the United States is today.

While most experts conclude that the geopolitical implications of aging in the developed world will be negative, a growing school of thought says that the same trend in the developing world will be positive—so positive, in fact, that it will make up for the developed world's growing weakness. It won't matter if the developed countries can't fight a war, because demographic trends will render the rest of the world increasingly pacific [peaceful].

This argument is based on the well-established relationship between youthful age structures and violent conflict. Throughout history, people have observed that young men are responsible for most of the world's mayhem. Since the mid-1990s, a large body of research has confirmed the close statistical correlation between the likelihood of conflict, especially civil strife, and the size of a society's "youth bulge," which is typically defined as the ratio of youth aged 15 to 24 to the entire adult population aged 15 and over. In the early post-cold-war years, this research triggered alarm among Pentagon planners about how sizable youth bulges in much of the developing world posed significant threats to U.S. interests. But more recently, experts have begun pointing to the projected decline in youth bulges as a cause for optimism. With each passing decade, they say, the propensity of the typical developing country to engage in violence can be expected to decline.

The Flawed "Demographic Peace" Thesis

We have dubbed this argument the "demographic peace" thesis. In its most-basic form, it holds that the demographic transition, by bringing about an older age structure, will, wherever and whenever it occurs, also bring social and political stability—and ultimately democracy—in its wake; today's security threats, from terrorism to nuclear proliferation, are just one last speed bump on the road to a more-peaceful future.

Although the demographic-peace thesis may seem plausible, we believe that it is deeply flawed. The demographic-peace thesis fails to take into account the huge variation in the timing and pace of the demographic transition, which is leaving some of the developing world's poorest and least-stable countries with large and lingering youth bulges, even as it threatens to subject some of the most-successful countries to the stresses of premature aging. It tends to focus exclusively on the threat of state failure, as in the Somalia model, while ignoring the threat of neoauthoritarian-state success, seen in the China or Russia model, which is more likely to occur in societies where the transition is already well under way.

More fundamentally, the demographic-peace thesis lacks any realistic sense of historical process. Rapid demographic change, when coupled with rapid development, can itself become a highly destabilizing force. As the developing world's demographic transition unfolds, it is deracinating traditional communities, overturning established economic and social relationships and cultural norms, and fueling a rising tide of ethnic strife and religious extremism. This hardly portends a new era of international peace. It is possible (though by no means assured) that the global security environment that emerges after the demographic transition has run its course will be safer than today's. It is very unlikely, however, that the transition will make the security environment progressively safer along the way.

Youth and Violence Still Hold Sway

Let's begin with the transition's very uneven progress. Averages can be misleading. Although it is true that the developing world as a whole is gradually aging, some of the poorest and least-stable nations are not aging at all. In sub-Saharan Africa, burdened by the world's highest fertility rates and ravaged by AIDS (which decimates the ranks of older adults), the average youth bulge is now 36 percent, more than twice the developed-world average. That share will remain practically unchanged over the next twenty-five years. The transition has also failed to gain traction in parts of the Muslim world, including Afghanistan, Iraq, the Palestinian territories, Somalia, Sudan and Yemen. Here fertility rates still tower in the 4–7 range—and youth bulges will linger at or near sub-Saharan African levels for decades to come. Most of these countries have amply demonstrated the correlation between extreme youth and violence in recent decades. If the correlation endures, chronic unrest could persist in much of sub-Saharan Africa and parts of the Muslim world through at least the 2030s.

Meanwhile, many of the developing world's most-rapidly modernizing nations are undergoing the full population shift from young and growing to old and declining at a breathtaking pace—far more rapidly than any of today's developed countries did. The adherents of the demographic-peace thesis apparently do not consider this to be a problem. But in fact, demographic transitions that proceed too fast or too far may turn out to be just as dangerous as stalled transitions.

Take China. With its sudden introduction of a one-child policy in the 1970s, China is now aging rapidly and faces a massive age wave that will arrive in the 2020s just as it is becoming a middle-income country. China has been "peacefully rising" while demographic trends have reinforced economic growth. But by the 2020s, the social and economic stresses triggered by its premature aging will be weakening the two pillars of the current regime's legitimacy: social stability and rapidly rising living standards.

Russia, another country undergoing an extreme demographic transition, must cope with a rate of population decline that literally has no historical precedent absent pandemic. By midcentury, its population will contract by one-third, dropping beneath 100 million. This would constitute a spectacular slide in Russia's world population ranking, from fourth place in 1950 to twentieth place in 2050. When a nation feels imperiled, it may reach for illiberal solutions—and when its geopolitical ambitions are threatened, it may act unpredictably. Russia's demographic future certainly does not square well with its geopolitical ambitions, and its leaders know it. While still president, Prime Minister Vladimir Putin, citing the nation's future economic and security needs, flatly declared Russia's birth dearth to be "the most-acute problem facing our nation today."

Echo-Booms

The majority of developing countries—in the rest of the Muslim world, in South Asia and in Latin America—lie somewhere in the middle. Their demographic transitions are neither stalled nor extreme. Their youth bulges are now declining rapidly, as the demographic-peace thesis predicts, while their future age waves are relatively small and lie far over the horizon. Yet here too, the transition is fraught with danger.

To begin with, the transition's impact in these regions is nonlinear. Many countries where youth bulges are now declining will experience a temporary resurgence in the number of young people in the 2020s. Demographers are familiar with this kind of "echo boom": it is an aftershock of the demographic transition. When rapid population growth is followed by a sudden population bust, it causes a ripple effect, with a gradually fading cycle of echo booms and busts that recurs every twenty to twenty-five years. A bust generation is now coming of age in much of Latin America, South Asia and the Muslim world. But by the 2020s, a large echo-boom generation will follow. As it does, the rate of growth in youth populations, which is now slowing in all of these regions, will suddenly reverse direction.

The echo booms of the 2020s will be largest in precisely those countries where fertility has fallen the fastest over the past twenty to twenty-five years and where youth bulges are therefore receding the most rapidly—that is, in precisely those countries where the demographic-peace thesis predicts that the impact of demographic trends will be the most positive. In Iran, whose fertility rate has plunged from 6.6 to 2.1 since 1980, the number of youth in the volatile 15–24 age bracket is due to contract by 34 percent between 2005 and 2020. But between 2020 and 2030, the number will once again surge by 30 percent. Many other Muslim-majority countries, from Libya to Pakistan, will also experience huge, regime-rocking oscillations in their youth populations.

Few of the demographic-peace theorists have noticed these echo booms. If asked to comment on them, most would no doubt say that, despite the roller-coaster ride, the long-term trend in youth bulges is downward in all of these countries— and that it is reasonable to expect that the twin forces of demographic aging and economic development will render them steadily more peaceful and democratic over time. But even here, the school is on shaky ground.

Historical Trends

This brings us to the most-serious weakness of the demographic-peace thesis—its lack of any realistic sense of historical process. Just because the present-day developed countries, which have completed the demographic transition, are relatively peaceful and democratic does *not* mean that today's developing countries, en route to completion, will become steadily more peaceful and democratic. Journeys can be much more dangerous than destinations. We have in fact only one historical example of a large group of countries that has completed the entire demographic transition—the family of today's (mostly Western) developed nations. And their experience during that transition, from the late 1700s to the late

1900s, was filled with the most-destructive revolutions, civil wars, total wars and genocides in the history of civilization. The nations that engaged in World War II had a higher average age and a lower fertility rate—and thus were situated at a later stage of the demographic transition—than most of today's developing world is projected to have over the next twenty years. If demographic aging breeds peace, in other words, we are not out of the woods yet.

Indeed, the potential threats to global security are likely to grow, not diminish, as the developing world's demographic transition gathers momentum. It is true that there is a broad correlation between youth and poverty on the one hand and chronic violence, social instability and civil war on the other. But upon closer examination, researchers are finding that the most-serious types of security threats actually describe a hump-shaped curve or "inverted-U" that initially rises along with economic development, whose speed and timing themselves tend to closely track the demographic transition in each country. In other words, the most-serious security threats are posed neither by the very youngest and poorest countries nor by the very oldest and richest, but rather by countries that are in the midst of the transition and the midst of development.

There is considerable evidence for a hump-shaped relationship between development and armed conflict in general. Looking at data on all armed conflicts between 1946 and 2006, the Center for Systemic Peace finds a clear inverted-U pattern, with countries in the second income quintile registering the highest magnitudes of warfare. As the center goes on to explain, this may be because "they have more capacity than countries in the bottom quintile to make war but less capacity than the upper quintiles to manage conflict." Other studies, covering different time periods stretching back a century or more, reach a similar conclusion.

This hump-shaped relationship appears to be even stronger for the most-serious types of security risks. Academic scholarship confirms what even the most-casual review of twentieth-century history suggests: the threats of interstate war, social revolution and genocide peak late in the transition. It is also well documented that international terrorism, among the developing countries, is positively correlated with income, education and urbanization. States that sponsor terrorism are rarely among the poorest countries; nor do the terrorists themselves usually originate in the poorest countries. Indeed, they are often disaffected members of the middle class in middle-income countries—as confirmed in remarkable detail by the recently discovered recruitment records of 606 foreign fighters who joined [global terrorist organization] al-Qaeda in Iraq between August 2006 and August 2007. This hump-shaped relationship is perhaps the strongest of all for neoauthoritarian consolidation and reaction, which is a far-greater threat in rapidly developing Iran, Russia or China than it is in sub-Saharan Africa.

Aggravating Stressors

None of this should be surprising given what we know about development. Economists, sociologists and historians who have studied the process agree that societies are buffeted by disorienting economic, social and cultural trends as they move from the traditional to the modern. When plotted against development, most of these trends themselves describe an inverted-U—meaning that they become most dangerous midway through the transition. Among the most-important stressors: contact with the global marketplace and global culture, urbanization, income inequality, ethnic strife, religious extremism and environmental degradation.

A few of these stressors bear some explanation. Perhaps the most-durable explanation of how inequality shifts over time was posited by economist Simon Kuznets over a half century ago. Inequality almost everywhere seems to move through distinct historical stages: it is low in traditional societies, rises rapidly with the onset of economic growth, then levels off and eventually falls as societies become capable of mass affluence. As inequality grows, some segments of the population experience what social scientists call "relative deprivation." The sense of deprivation is intensified by growing mobility, urbanization and exposure to the mass media, which make people more acutely sensitive to differences in relative living standards. This dynamic helps to explain why most of history's great social upheavals have occurred not in static agrarian societies, but in societies (like France in 1789 or Russia in 1917) where incomes—and inequality—were growing rapidly.

Ethnic strife is another factor that can lead to a bumpy ride on the way to stability. In most societies, some ethnic groups are more successful in the marketplace than others—which means that as development accelerates and the market economy grows, rising inequality often falls along ethnic lines. In *World on Fire*, Yale professor of law Amy Chua documents how the concentration of wealth among "market-dominant minorities" has triggered violent backlashes by majority populations in many developing countries, from Indonesia, Malaysia and the Philippines (against the Chinese) to Sierra Leone (against the Lebanese) to the former Yugoslavia (against the Croats and Slovenes). The likelihood of conflict grows not just with development, but with democratization. As Chua observes, the sudden political empowerment of poor, disenfranchised majorities can give rise to "powerful ethnonationalist, anti-market pressures and routinely results in confiscation, instability, authoritarian backlash, and violence."

Finally, consider religious extremism. Many suppose that the appeal of radical Islam will diminish as development reduces poverty, raises educational attainment and integrates societies into the global marketplace. But in fact, like the surging growth of fundamentalist Christianity in sub-Saharan Africa, Latin America and East Asia, the rise of radical Islam is in

Cartoon by Eldon Pletcher. www.cartoonstock.com.

large part a reaction to modernization. Religious- and cultural-revitalization movements help to fill the void that is left behind as development uproots communities and fragments extended families. They also reaffirm traditional cultural identities that are threatened by modernization—which is to say, the onslaught of Western values. In the case of radical Islam, the backlash has of course led to violent confrontation with the West. The forces fueling the reaction are unlikely to abate—and indeed may intensify—as the transition progresses.

The stresses triggered by the demographic transition help to explain the fragility of so many new democracies. When social scientists sort regimes by likelihood of violent conflict, which type do they find is most at risk? Not traditional autocratic regimes, virtually all of which are found in societies at the beginning of the transition. And not fully developed liberal democracies, virtually all of which are found in societies where the transition has long since been completed. Rather, it is semidemocracies, or "anocracies," virtually all of which are found in societies that are in the midst of the transition and the midst of development. Much research confirms that the frequency and intensity of state-organized violence exhibits an inverted-U relationship to regime type. Political-scientist Ian Bremmer calls this the "J curve"—the tendency of openness and democracy to make states less stable before it makes them more stable. . . .

Between Autocracy and Chaos

Any realistic assessment of future geopolitical threats must acknowledge that the greatest dangers to security over the next few decades lie not in very young countries, but in countries where the transition is well under way. Although many of the youth-bulge countries in sub-Saharan Africa and the Muslim world are likely to remain "trouble spots," most of the trouble will not have geopolitical repercussions—except when it involves terrorism or interferes with the flow of important natural resources.

What we need to worry most about are large and rapidly developing countries that could either slip into chaos or else become affluent, technologically advanced and civically cohesive, yet hostile to liberal democracy. State failure in Iran or Pakistan, to say nothing of Russia or China, would clearly have far-more-dangerous regional and global consequences than state failure in a Somalia or Sierra Leone. By the same token, so would the consolidation of neoauthoritarian regimes as their economics become fully developed. Although the faster-transitioning countries of the developing world may experience less chronic violence than the countries with large and persistent youth bulges, the crises that they do experience will tend to be more serious. Their economies are more productive, their governments are better financed, their militaries are better armed and their rival factions are better organized. Several have nuclear weapons. Many stand on the knife-edge between civil chaos and one-party autocracy. In their demographic and economic development, most have entered the phase of maximum danger and must therefore be watched closely.

> *"In Western countries, the combination of a sharp decline in the birth rates of the European or European-descended population . . . and the sharp increase in the non-European immigrant population . . . is bringing about a major transformation in military strategy."*

Declining Birthrates in Developed Countries Are Changing Military Strategy

James Kurth

In the following viewpoint, James Kurth, a professor of political science at Swarthmore College in Pennsylvania, claims that declining birthrates in Europe, the United States, and China will lead to fewer military recruits and thus smaller armies. To Kurth, this means these powers will lose their military edge as the citizens will not wish the fewer young people sacrificed needlessly in wars. Ultimately, for Kurth, this implies that these military superpowers will refrain from engaging with nations with nuclear weapons as well as nations with dedicated guerrilla armies that can protract warfare for decades. Although some might see this as a benefit to global peace, Kurth believes that demographic

James Kurth, "One-Child Foreign Policy," *American Conservative*, vol. 6, no. 16, August 27, 2007, pp. 6–10.

*shifts in populations within Western states will eventually re-
quire the military to consider devising strategies to hold back
minority insurgencies. However, since minorities are still enjoying high birthrates, Kurth believes these strategies can only delay
the inevitable internal fragmentation of these powerful nations.*

As you read, consider the following questions:

1. According to Kurth, how is RAM affecting attitudes toward warfare and the military?

2. What types of nations does the author say the United
   States will be ideally prepared to fight in coming years?

3. What demographic group does Kurth believe will create
   a "second civilization" in the industrialized powers of
   Europe?

Military analysts are always talking about strategy. Often
they are proposing one that they have just invented and
naturally think will be the solution to the nation's security
problems. The present time, filled as it is with the threat of Islamist terrorism and with the debacle of the Iraq War, is especially marked by the proliferation of strategic proposals.

More seasoned analysts know, however, that if any strategy
is to prove effective, it must fit social and structural realities,
including the state of technology, the economy, and the political system. Less noted is the role of demography.

Until recently, demographic changes were so slow that
they hardly seemed to be a variable affecting strategic challenges. But today, many major nations are undergoing rapid
and evident changes in their demographic structure. This is
most obvious in Europe, but it is also the case in the United
States, Russia, China, and Japan. Demographic disruption is
impacting America, all of its major allies, and all of its traditional or potential adversaries.

The Graying of the West

In Western countries, the combination of a sharp decline in the birth rates of the European or European-descended population, on the one hand, and the sharp increase in the non-European immigrant population, on the other, is causing a great transformation in social structure and national identity, which is bringing about a major transformation in military strategy. The process has only begun, but in the years ahead, history will teach us once again that demography is destiny.

In order for a particular population to sustain its numbers, it should have an average reproduction rate of 2.1 births per woman. But the birth rate for almost every Western nation has fallen below 1.5 during the last couple of decades. In Italy and Spain, formerly the European nations with the highest birth rates, it is now under 1.3. Although the United States has a rising population, that growth is entirely due to immigration and to the higher reproduction rates of peoples of non-European origin. With the exception of devout religious communities—especially the Mormons—among most European-American groups, reproduction rates are below the level of sustainability.

When one projects these demographic statistics forward, it appears inevitable that in half a century most European-descended peoples will have only two-thirds or less of the population that they have today. Furthermore, a much larger percentage of that population will be old and no longer able to work. It follows that national security will have a very different meaning when nations themselves have become so different.

Revising Strategies

A transformation in Western, particularly American, military strategy has occurred alongside this demographic transformation. New technologies have issued in great improvements in what the military calls C4—command, control, communication, and computers. In the past two decades, the U.S. military has found it essential to incorporate these improvements into its strategies, operations, and weapons acquisitions, with the totality of results being called the "revolution in military affairs" or RMA.

Unfortunately, there is always someone who will carry a good thing too far, as was the case with former Defense Secretary Donald Rumsfeld's ineffective "military transformation" project. Rumsfeld's misuse of the RMA meant reducing the size of the U.S. ground forces, but it had always been focused upon enabling our military to defeat other militaries—that is to say, upon conventional war—and had nothing to say about defeating insurgencies, as has become amply clear in Iraq. Rumsfeld's reductions made the transformed ground forces even less capable of dealing with the Iraqi insurgency than the old-fashioned pre-transformation forces would have been.

There has also been a parallel "revolution in attitudes toward the military" or RAM. Whereas the RMA has principally been propelled by the new technologies of the information economy, the RAM has been driven by the new demography of low birth rates. These two revolutions are connected and mutually reinforcing.

In the modernizing societies of a century ago, the number of children per couple was normally four or more. It was also common for some of these children to die from disease while their parents were still living. If it happened that some instead died while fighting in a war, this was seen as a sad, but not surprising, variation on the familiar theme of death among the young.

Today, it is very rare for a child in postmodern society to die from disease while his parents are alive. And if he should die in military combat, this is seen as a shocking surprise. Indeed, for one of these rare children to die in such a rare way will increasingly seem a unique catastrophe and an unacceptable scandal. This is particularly true for the children of the professional class—the liberal professionals and the professional liberals. This class, of course, is especially large and dominant in the information economy and postmodern culture.

The "Low-Casualty" Imperative

It is difficult to imagine such a society, with its one-child demography and no-death mentality, undertaking such military operations as the massive infantry assaults and trench warfare of World War I, the immense amphibious invasions and foxhole fighting of World War II, and the prolonged and stalemated combat of the Korean War. These kinds of operations could be undertaken by a modern society, but they probably are beyond the capabilities of a postmodern one. The popular opposition to the prolonged combat of the Vietnam War and now the Iraq War illustrates the point. Rather, the military undertakings that are suitable for a postmodern society are the highly mobile and extremely brief operations of the Persian Gulf War and the Kosovo War. Above all, they must be low-casualty operations. (During the Kosovo War, NATO [North Atlantic Treaty Organization, a U.S.–Western European military alliance,] forces did not suffer a single combat death.)

This low-casualty imperative is the major feature of the revolution in attitudes toward the military. It obviously has a major impact, and imposes major limitations, upon strategy, especially the strategy of the U.S. Army. It is also a major factor promoting the revolution in military affairs, as the United States once again, as it has in earlier wars, seeks to use high technologies to ensure low casualties. This is especially the case with the strategy of the U.S. Air Force.

In the aftermath of their dismal Iraq experience, American ground forces, especially the Army, will very likely want to avoid counterinsurgency wars. After the Vietnam War, the Army tried to reinvent itself in a way that would make it difficult for civilian policymakers to put it into a war involving guerrillas or insurgents. The famous Weinberger-Powell Doctrine, which in effect proscribed prolonged counterinsurgency wars, was one result. The Air-Land Battle Doctrine, which provided for high-tech wars against conventional armies, was another. After the Iraq War, the Army will probably turn to some new high-tech variation of its conventional definition and mission and therefore to some new version of the RMA to correct the distorted version of the Rumsfeld era. Moreover, the post-Iraq and neo-RMA Army will have to operate within the context of a widespread popular resistance to military casualties, which will be even greater than it was before the Iraq War—a sort of neo-RAM.

What strategy will the Army develop in response to the double impact of the post-Iraq versions of the RMA and the RAM? What kind of enemies will the Army want to fight so that it can use high technology to fight its wars, while keeping American casualties low?

An Army Without an Enemy

On the one hand, it is clear that the Army will not want to fight guerrillas or insurgents, and therefore it will not really develop a counterinsurgency strategy. Most of the current Army's focus upon counterinsurgency strategy will disappear soon after it withdraws from Iraq, rather like its elaborate, if short-lived, efforts at counterinsurgency strategy made during the Vietnam War. On the other hand, it is also clear that the Army will not want to fight the conventional forces of America's most obvious peer competitor, China.

The kind of enemies that the Army will want to fight will be something in between: the conventional forces of medium or small-size powers—what have often been called rogue states. But the Army will want to be sure that these enemies' conventional forces do not turn into counterinsurgencies, as happened in Iraq. Indeed, in the months before the Iraq War began, the Army was concerned about this very possibility.

That is why the Army chief of staff, Gen. Eric Shinseki, wanted several hundred thousand soldiers to impose order in post-Saddam Iraq and to abort an insurgency before it could develop. Still earlier, and because of the same concern, the Army had been very cautious about sending ground troops into Kosovo in 1999. (It was the good fortune of the Army—and of the [President Bill] Clinton administration—that Serbia capitulated before NATO ground forces had to be employed.)

Given all of these constraints, there are not really that many enemies left for the U.S. Army to fight. The [George W.] Bush administration's 2002 list of rogue states—the notorious "axis of evil"—specified Iraq, Iran, and North Korea. But given what has happened in Iraq, it is unlikely that the Army will want to fight in Iran; it not only looks too much like Iraq, but is three times as big. As for North Korea, the Army has long been prepared to fight a conventional, high-tech campaign against that country's conventional, low-tech army. But North Korea is now not just a conventional power; it is potentially a nuclear one. If even the Bush administration has proved reluctant to use military force against North Korea, it is almost certain that any future administration will be reluctant, too.

It thus appears that the Army is left with no specific and identifiable enemy. The most that it will be able to contemplate is some hypothetical, conventional rogue state that may materialize sometime in the future—which makes it difficult to develop a credible strategy. . . .

Declining Births and Foreign Armies

China, like the U.S., is also characterized by a sharp decline in its birth rate, which will affect its military strategy. China's lowered birth rate, of course, is not a result of postmodern values—it is still a modernizing society, although one with substantial modern sectors—but of the government's one-child policy. And like the United States, China has undertaken

The Decline of the White US Majority

The census calculates that by 2042, Americans who identify themselves as Hispanic, black, Asian, American Indian, Native Hawaiian and Pacific Islander will together outnumber non-Hispanic whites. [In 2004], officials had projected the shift would come in 2050.

Sam Roberts, New York Times, *August 14, 2008.*

its own version of military transformation. It has substantially reduced the numbers of its infantry soldiers and is developing an impressive capability to use high technologies for military purposes, especially for cyberwar. China seeks to trump the U.S. advantage in capital-intensive, high-tech weapons systems, particularly aircraft carriers and fighter bombers, by leaping over these to a new, information-age version of asymmetrical warfare.

(There is one peculiar twist to China's low birth rate. Because of the traditional preference for male children, the government's one-child policy often becomes a one-boy, no-girl practice. Some Chinese provinces now have as many as 120 or more boys for every 100 girls. As these excess boys reach late adolescence, the age of both high youth-crime rates and high army-recruitment rates, maintaining internal stability may require the civilizing influence of military discipline, leading it to maintain a large army despite depressed birth rates.)

Russia has been afflicted with the greatest decline in birth rate of any major power in the past two decades. For this reason, but also because of economic constraints and bureaucratic corruption and incompetence, the Russian Army has become hollow. Russia has many grievances against several of its neighbors, which were once republics within the Soviet Union and are now within Russia's "near abroad." But its army is not a very effective instrument for the Kremlin to use in dealing with these grievances. Instead, it has turned to non-military instruments, such as cutting off vital oil and natural gas exports or, recently, cyberwar attacks on Estonia's vital government and financial computer systems. Russia's low birth rate means that its army probably will be weak for years to come.

Shifting Military Focus

It might thus seem that the consequences of demographic change are rather benign, at least with respect to the prospects for greater international peace and tranquility. America's historical and potential peer competitors and military rivals are less likely to engage in aggression because they lack the large reserves of surplus manpower that were so much a part of their military pasts. And America itself will be less likely to undertake foreign wars and military adventures, not only because of the short-term consequences of its debacle in Iraq but also because of the long-term effects of its low birth rate and the low-casualty imperative. From a traditional conservative perspective, with its emphasis on the prudent, sensible, and realistic use of military force, the era of low birth rates among the major powers might seem to be a good thing.

Unfortunately, when we turn our attention from the international arena to the domestic one, and from military strategy to internal security, a very different picture emerges. Particularly in the West, radical demographic change means that the prospect for greater peace and tranquility abroad is dialectically and diabolically connected to the prospect for greater conflict and violence at home.

Current social attitudes and demographic trends in the West suggest that there will be a continuation of low reproduction rates among Western peoples and therefore a severe decline in their populations. Conversely, there will be a continuation of high immigration of non-Western peoples into the Western nations and of higher reproduction rates among the non-Western communities in the West than among the Western peoples themselves. This will have major consequences not only for the military strategies of the Western nations but for their national security—and even identity.

Insurgencies in the Making

The most dramatic consequences are likely to occur in Europe, where most of the non-Western populations will be Muslim. These communities already perform functions essential to the economic system, and within the next decade, they are poised to become an important part of the political system. Many European countries will become two nations, and Europe as a whole will become two civilizations. The first will be a Western civilization or, more accurately, given Europeans' rejection of many Western traditions, a post-Western civilization comprised of people of European descent. It will be secular, even pagan, rich, old, and feeble. The second will be the non-Western civilization, descended from non-European peoples. It will be religious, even Islamic, poor, young, and vigorous. It will be a kind of overseas colony of a foreign civilization, a familiar occurrence in European history, but this time the foreign civilization will be the *umma* [community or "church"] of Islam and the colonized country will be Europe itself. The two civilizations will regard each other with mutual contempt. In the new civilization, there will be a growing rage, and in the old civilization, there will be a growing fear. These will be the perfect conditions for endemic Islamic terrorism, urban riots, and mob violence: an Islamist insurgency within Europe itself.

Analogous, but less dramatic, developments are likely to occur in the United States. Here the most numerous of the non-Western communities will be Latin American in their origin. Latino immigrants already perform functions essential to the American economic system and are steadily acquiring political power, including a kind of veto on many issues. It is possible that the United States might also become two nations or even two civilizations, although this is not as likely as in Europe. It is probably too much to predict that in the Anglo nation there will be a widespread fear of some kind of Latino terrorism, although young Latinos in the United States may learn from their Islamic counterparts in Europe. It is quite plausible, however, that there will be Latino urban riots and mob violence. And it is very likely that there will be a widespread fear of Latino crime. Gated communities, which are already widespread in the southwestern United States, could become an even more central part of the Anglo way of life, the distinctive architectural style and urban design of the Anglo nation.

Holding Together Divided Nations

Is there any kind of strategy that can deal effectively with the kind of internal violence and insecurity that many Western nations will face in the future?

On the one hand, this challenge is obviously not one of traditional war against a foreign military, so conventional military strategies will not be applicable. Neither is it defined by sporadic attacks by small, separated terrorist groups, so standard counterterrorist strategies are also inapplicable. What we face instead are episodic and perhaps endemic terrorist attacks and violence perpetrated by a minority supported by a much larger community hostile toward the majority society. Such a condition is normally called insurgency or, if it reaches a large enough scale, civil war.

European nations could experience in their homelands and from a Muslim minority of 10 percent or more a version of what France experienced in its Algerian colony from a

Muslim majority of 90 percent. And the European population will have no place to retreat to. The Basque guerrillas in Spain, the Tamil Tigers in Sri Lanka, and the Muslim insurgents in India (Kashmir) are largely concentrated in a particular territory, making territorial secession seem like a viable objective. That is not the case with the Muslim community within Europe.

In the past, a minority community that turned militant has almost always been confronted with a majority that also became militant. In short, the majority had enough sense of being a community that it could come together, bring its weight to bear, and put down the militant minority. Effective and appropriate tactics have included arresting and imprisoning some of the minority's leaders and co-opting or isolating the rest, and, if there has been another minority community, setting it against the militant one. And from time to time, violent young men of the majority have engaged in their own mob violence against the minority. This has wonderfully concentrated the mind of the minority community and usually resulted in its becoming more prudent. Of course, in our era of low birth rates, there are not that many young men of the majority around.

When a militant, violent minority community confronts a militant, violent majority community, the outcome will be clear—so clear that the minority is usually sensible enough not to become militant and violent in the first place. The outcome is less certain when a minority community confronts a majority that is only one in the numerical sense—just a conglomeration of little groups and isolated individuals who define themselves by ideologies like multiculturalism, diversity, or expressive individualism.

For the nations of the West, which have arrived at this historically unprecedented state, a viable strategy for the nation is no longer really possible because they are no longer really nations at all.

> "The growth in population ... is re-
> sponsible for more than half of urban
> growth."

Population Growth Is Leading to Increased Urbanization

Leiwen Jiang, Malea Hoepf Young, and Karen Hardee

In the following viewpoint, Leiwen Jiang, Malea Hoepf Young, and Karen Hardee examine the costs of a rapidly urbanizing global population. Assuming that the number of city dwellers will double by the year 2050, Jiang, Young, and Hardee predict that ecosystems will suffer as surface temperatures, water use, and greenhouse gas emissions all rise. Although the authors maintain that urbanization may also lead to improved access to medical care and better economic opportunities for those flocking to cities, they fear that unless cities are capable of providing needed services to so many people, urban areas could become dens of poverty and environmental blight. Leiwen Jiang is a senior demographer in the research division of Population Action International, a nonprofit family planning and global health organization. Malea Hoepf Young is a research associate with the same organization, as is Karen Hardee, who is the vice president of research.

Leiwen Jiang, Malea Hoepf Young, and Karen Hardee, "Population, Urbanization, and the Environment," *World Watch*, vol. 21, no. 5, September/October 2008, pp. 34–39.

As you read, consider the following questions:

1. According to UN predictions cited by the authors, what will be the global urban population in 2050?

2. As Jiang, Young, and Hardee report, what percentage of African city dwellers live in informal settlements (slums) attached to urban centers?

3. According to the authors, which produce more carbon per energy unit consumed—low-income countries or high-income countries?

People have been moving from the countryside to the city for at least 9,000 years, but this key population trend has now become one of the most visible and profound forces on Earth: 2008 is the first year in which more than half of us have become city dwellers. The process of becoming a mainly urban species has accelerated during the past century and has now concentrated nearly three-and-a-half billion people on less than 3 percent of the planet's land surface. These monumental agglomerations of people, buildings, factories, roads, and vehicles—along with their associated social systems—have manifold and powerful environmental impacts, as well as effects on fertility and population growth rates, that we are only beginning to understand.

The urbanization trend is global, but rates of urbanization have varied significantly by country and region. The world's more developed countries (as classified by the United Nations) were predominantly urban by the 1950s, but the group of less developed countries is not projected to reach this point until 2019, with some important regional and country variations.

Global Urban Population Will Double

Between 2007 and 2050, the UN projects that global population will increase by 2.5 billion (from 6.7 to 9.2 billion), while the global urban population will nearly double (from 3.3 billion to 6.4 billion), absorbing all increased population growth as well as inflows from rural areas. This enormous increase in the global urban population will be greater than the current populations of China, India, the United States, Indonesia, and Mexico combined. Further, this increase will be concentrated in the developing world, particularly in Asia and Africa. While developing countries will continue to be predominantly rural for some years to come, they are already home to over 70 percent of the global urban population, a proportion that will increase in the coming decades to over 80 percent by 2050. In contrast, the urban population of the highly urbanized developed countries represents less than 30 percent of global total, and its share will drop to less than 20 percent by 2050.

The world's urban dwellers live in many different types of cities. Megacities—those with over 10 million inhabitants, such as New York, Shanghai, Tokyo, Bombay, and Mexico City—make up 9 percent of the global urban population. However, 52 percent of the world's urban population lives in cities with fewer than 500,000 inhabitants, although the bottom threshold for an urban designation varies by country.

It is commonly perceived that urbanization and urban growth are driven by waves of international and rural-urban migration. However, natural increase (the growth in population resulting from a higher rate of births than deaths) is responsible for more than half of urban growth, with the reclassification of rural areas to urban ones contributing to urbanization as well. This natural increase is significant even though fertility rates are nearly always lower in urban than rural areas, influenced by the higher costs of childrearing in urban areas and the lesser need for children's household labor (e.g., for tending to fields or livestock). The trend toward lower fertility rates is further accelerated by increased economic opportunities for women, increased access to education, and greater access to family planning and reproductive health services. For example, urban fertility rates in Kenya,

187

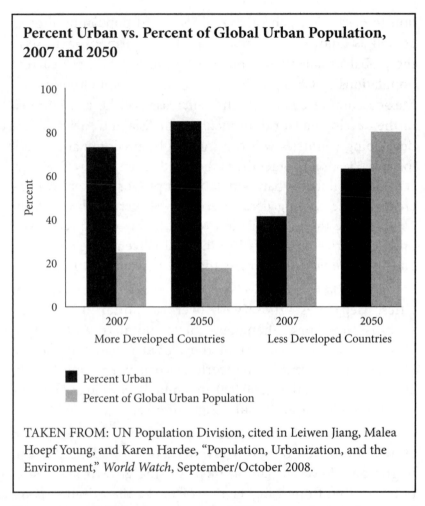

Percent Urban vs. Percent of Global Urban Population, 2007 and 2050

TAKEN FROM: UN Population Division, cited in Leiwen Jiang, Malea Hoepf Young, and Karen Hardee, "Population, Urbanization, and the Environment," *World Watch*, September/October 2008.

Tanzania, and Uganda are around 40 percent lower than rural rates, and well below the national averages. However, all are above replacement level (the average number of births per woman at which population growth stabilizes, i.e., 2.1), and in Uganda, urban women bear over four children on average, contributing to the rapid growth of its urban centers.

Impact on Ecosystems

Growing cities inflict profound changes on their local environments. The most well-documented change is the urban heat-island effect, which results in cities tending to have higher air and surface temperatures than their rural surroundings, especially at night. City size, land cover patterns (increased area covered with buildings, roads, and other surfaces impervious to water, and reduced area covered by vegetation and water), and the canyon-like heat-trapping capabilities of high-rise buildings all contribute to the formation of heat-island effects. These effects have impacts on water resources, biodiversity, air flow and quality, and ecosystem functioning, all of which can cause formation of smog and promote dispersion of pollutants.

Urbanization also alters the circulation and conservation of water. Throughout history, cities have been constructed along rivers, deltas, and coastlines, which provide water sources, transportation routes, and power. These water sources have been modified to meet urban needs, often at the expense of local aquatic ecosystems, which help protect from natural disasters. In India and Sri Lanka, for example, depleted mangrove forests left coastal communities vulnerable to the 2005 tsunami, while communities where those ecosystems remained intact fared much better.

Concentration of transportation and industry in urban areas also modifies biogeochemical cycles, or the flow of chemical elements and compounds. Cities concentrate sources of CO_2 [carbon dioxide] and other greenhouse gases and pollutants, which influence neighboring ecosystems. In the natural environment, accumulated air pollutants are removed as rainwater washes the air and then filters into the groundwater table, but in urban areas the pollutants run off the impervious surfaces and wash directly into rivers, streams, and oceans. The preponderance of cities along rivers and coastlines makes urban areas important contributors to the eutrophication (increase in chemical nutrients) of water bodies, which can reduce water quality and damage marine ecosystems.

Urbanization also fragments natural spaces and threatens biodiversity, as expanding cities exert pressure on ecosystems on the fringe of urban areas. However, rural-to-rural migration, including movement to remote areas, forest frontiers, and coastal areas with greater land and resource availability, is often more harmful to biodiversity.

The growth rates of many cities in developing countries stress the ability of local governments to enforce environmental protections and cope with increased demands on related infrastructure. Most developing countries undergoing rapid urbanization do not have the resources to detect many modern chemicals or to establish facilities to treat hazardous wastes. In those cities, stormwater infrastructures often do not separate storm runoff from wastewater discharges, creating acute pollution problems in recipient waterways. Many cities have inadequate waste management policies and practices, even though solid-waste management accounts for 20 to 50 percent of local government spending in developing countries.

Informal settlements and slums (which house over 1 billion of the world's urban dwellers) are often unconnected to even basic sanitation systems; in some African cities over 90 percent of the urban population lives in such areas. Rivers and canals in developing country cities often function as large open sewers. Sixty percent of rivers flowing through Chinese cities, for example, do not meet minimum drinking-water standards.

Air pollution from vehicles, industry, and households often exceeds the natural environment's ability to cope with it. Although automotive lead emissions have declined sharply in most developed countries, they are generally rising in developing countries, particularly in the very largest cities of some Asian countries that use leaded gasoline and have no plans to phase it out. Moreover, emissions of automotive sulfur dioxide, particulate matter, and lead are likely to be significantly higher in the future because of increasing car ownership in many cities—enabled by the introduction of cheap cars such as the Indian automaker Tata Motors' "Nano," whose US$2,500 price tag makes it affordable to the country's growing middle class—as well as the more extensive use of diesel-powered vehicles and poor quality automotive fuel.

Urbanization's Benefits

While urbanization is often blamed for environmental harm, cities offer many potential benefits, including some that can be environmentally benign or helpful. In much of the world, and in all countries that have attained high income levels, urbanization and economic growth have gone hand in hand. Technical innovation, access to information, efficient land and energy use, better living conditions, provision of clean water, and access to health care services can result from cities with good governance decentralized to the local level, and adequate funding for urban planning and infrastructure can lead to better quality of life for residents and reduced damage to the environment. Increasing economies of scale resulting from urbanization can reduce per-capita natural resource consumption compared with rural areas and smaller towns or cities. In New York, for example, per-capita greenhouse gas emissions are now just one-third of the U.S. average.

However, the relationship between urbanization and the environment is complex. Some economists argue that it changes over time: a growing economy, which often accompanies urbanization, leads to increased consumption and waste emissions. But when a certain level of wealth is achieved, waste emissions tend to decline. The formal statement of this theory is called the environmental Kuznets curve, a bell-shaped curve that shows waste emission and pollution increasing with income in the early stages of industrialization and urbanization, but declining after reaching a certain threshold due to more efficient resource use and improved waste treatment. This theory has held for water pollution and some air pollutants (such as sulfur dioxide and soot), which directly affect local urban environments. However, the relationship becomes less clear when the impacts, such as biodiversity loss and global climate change, occur beyond local areas.

The environmental Kuznets curve phenomenon does play out in one study of urbanization and energy use in 237 countries between 1980 and 2005. After controlling for the income level of the countries, the analysis of relationships among urbanization, energy consumption, and carbon emissions showed that countries with higher levels of urbanization (as observed in virtually all high- and middle-income countries) have economies with high energy intensity (energy consumed to produce a unit of GDP [gross domestic product]). However, these countries emit less carbon per unit of energy used (termed *carbon intensity*). This occurs even though this group includes nearly all the world's highest emitters. Economies of scale, technological advances in energy efficiency, and the adoption of cleaner fossil-fuel and alternative energy sources mitigate these nations' emissions, although their contributions remain immense. On the other hand, rapidly urbanizing countries (including many low-income countries, particularly in Africa and Asia) have less energy-intensive economies but emit more carbon for each unit of energy they consume. In effect, they are using "dirtier" energy, including burning coal and biomass.

The declines in fertility and slowed population growth associated with urbanization also have a complex relationship with the environment and emissions. In gross terms, fewer people mean fewer carbon emitters, and potentially less greenhouse gases in the atmosphere. However, per-capita carbon emissions vary widely across and within countries. A comparison of future population growth in India under different scenarios of urbanization found that by 2050 total population will be 20 percent less under a medium urbanization scenario (assuming a population that is 45 percent urban) than under a low urbanization scenario (which assumes a population that is 35 percent urban). However, higher consumption of fossil fuels in India will produce 25 percent more carbon dioxide emissions under the more urbanized scenario by year 2100.

These results do not mean that developing countries should reduce energy consumption. In India, a large percentage of the population still lives in severe energy poverty (83 percent of the urban population and only 49 percent of the rural population have access to electricity), which slows advances in economic and human development. Rather, the studies demonstrate the imperative of providing modern, clean, and affordable energy resources to meet India's and the rest of the world's growing demands.

Emissions Reduction

Urbanization is an inevitable, ongoing, and accelerating process, and almost all future population growth will occur in developing countries. Without significant and equitable economic growth to keep pace, the rapid urbanization of future populations will mean the urbanization of poverty—in that larger numbers and a larger percentage of the world's poor will live in urban areas—with cities in low-income countries increasingly afflicted with social and environmental ills. The relationships among urbanization, population growth, consumption, and environmental change are complex, and urbanization has both negative and positive aspects and consequences. Developed, largely urbanized countries are in a better position to achieve low carbon intensity by adopting new energy technologies, but some still lack the political will to do so, even as the impacts of climate change begin to unfold. On the other hand, developing countries with relatively high urban growth rates will increase their carbon emissions through increasing energy use, which will boost their economies and improve standards of living, and will also contribute to global greenhouse gas emissions. This raises difficult ethical questions of equity in emissions between rich and poor countries, at a time when it is urgent to drastically reduce global emissions. It also highlights the importance of transferring cleaner and more efficient technologies without hindering development.

> "Migrating masses, moving from one
> economic opportunity to another, [are]
> tied to very little but their religious
> faiths."

Migrant Populations Tend to Identify More with Their Religious Affiliations

Arun Pereira

In the viewpoint that follows, Arun Pereira, an associate professor of marketing at St. Louis University, asserts that in times of great migration brought on by changing economic and social conditions, religion has remained a powerful anchor for establishing identity. Pereira believes that in the modern era of globalization, this principle holds especially true. He claims migrants today are seeking new opportunities in wealthy nations, often changing the cultural character of those nations and refraining from assimilation. Clinging to their religion as a constant, these migrants form enclaves that owe loyalty only to their faith, Pereira states. He warns that these divisions could clash in the future either over scarce resources or the dissolution of superpowers that struggle to maintain some sort of national identity.

Arun Pereira, "The Rally Round Religion," *National Catholic Reporter*, vol. 44, no. 25, August 8, 2008, pp. 14–15.

As you read, consider the following questions:

1. According to the International Migration Organization cited by the author, about how many immigrants were there worldwide in 2005?

2. Under what coming circumstances does Pereira predict Western populations will start joining the migrating masses?

3. According to the author, what will be the "end result" of immigrants not assimilating into the national identity of their adopted lands?

A time of expanding global trade, new technologies disseminating information in unprecedented ways, and religious fanaticism forcing people to take up arms—yes, the 16th century was a momentous period that saw a surge in globalization, the invention of the printing press, and wars driven by religious fanatics. It also saw the unraveling of a unique alliance between the popes and the emperors, the so-called Holy Roman Empire, after eight centuries of mutually beneficial—and sometimes uneasy—collaboration. That alliance and its unraveling may have important implications for the present time, particularly as the world experiences unprecedented levels of immigration and grapples with difficult challenges in the assimilation of immigrants.

Religion as a Constant

Beginning with Charlemagne in A.D. 800, the emperors of the Holy Roman Empire used religion—through the papacy—to wield power over subjects spread over various principalities and fiefdoms in Western and Central Europe. Charlemagne and his successors were officially crowned by the popes, thereby bestowing a spiritual legitimacy to their reigns. In return, the pope received security and protection. The emperors recognized the power of religion to unify diverse subjects—

people of various ethnicities and social classes, speaking languages that varied from German and its dialects to the Slavic languages.

This strategy worked because Europe was going through a tumultuous period characterized by changing emperors and kings, shifting boundaries among fiefdoms, and people on the move. Under these ever-changing conditions, individual identity was shaped by the one constant in people's lives: religion. Allegiance to religion bested all other loyalties such as allegiance to emperors, barons, and even ethnicity, language and social class.

Today in most parts of the world people are undergoing unparalleled change, driven by the effects of globalization. We are witnessing the greatest wave of migration in the history of the world. According to the International Migration Organization, there were nearly 200 million immigrants worldwide in 2005, a number that equals the fifth-most populous country in the world. Even as we see efforts in the United States and Western Europe to deter illegal immigration, the forces of globalization are driving legal immigration to levels never seen before. Globalization is changing the structure of the world economy, with nation-states giving way to giant trade-blocs and national borders being redefined or erased. All these factors fundamentally undermine patriotism and national identity.

Maintaining Identity by Religion

People in the West may not appreciate or recognize this "identity crisis" because they have yet to fully experience the wrenching consequences of globalization affecting those in the developing world. Consider today's global immigrants. Where do the identity and allegiance of a new immigrant lie? Nation of birth? Nation of present residence? A giant trade-bloc? This is a crucial question because individual identity is fundamental to how conflicts start. According to Stanley Kober, a research fellow in foreign policy studies at the CATO Institute, "Wars begin in people's minds—and are rooted in how they view other people. Put simply, people do not kill people with whom they identify." In a borderless world wrought by continuous instability and change, with what or whom does one identify?

History would suggest that just like during the Holy Roman Empire, people's identities and loyalties are increasingly tied to the one constant in their lives: religion, be it one of the established faiths or otherwise. So much so, they are likely to put their lives on the line for religion more readily than for any other cause. As an example, Kober offers the breakup of Yugoslavia. Its citizens coalesced into countries based on religion: Muslim Bosnia, Orthodox Serbia, Catholic Croatia. More telling was the pattern of international sympathy for these new nations; Germany, the kingpin of the erstwhile Holy Roman Empire, led the way for the early recognition of Catholic Croatia, as did Greece and Russia for Orthodox Serbia, and a host of Islamic nations for Muslim Bosnia.

It is a matter of time before the full effects of this identity crisis hit the West. As national borders continue to fall and more trade blocs emerge, the people in the West will join the migrating masses, moving from one economic opportunity to another, tied to very little but their religious faiths. In the future, even if you don't move, much of the world's population will be doing so, fundamentally affecting you and forcing you to confront the basis of your national identity. We already see this in Europe where a growing Muslim population is causing Europeans to take a closer look at their Christian roots. In the United States, if non-European, non-Christian immigrants come in great numbers as they are already starting to do, many Americans will also feel a need to defend and emphasize the "Christian" identity of the United States. Americans will react like the rest of the world, rallying around their religious faith and fiercely protecting it. It may be the aspect of their identity that Americans prove unwilling to compromise on, even as they adapt to and tolerate the changing face of their country in terms of skin colors, languages and cultures. In the extreme, a "brown" America (or even a "Spanish" America) will likely be tolerated but not a Muslim America, or a Hindu America.

Faith Will Matter More than Flags

There is little incentive for today's immigrants to completely assimilate in the host country because their sheer numbers make it easier for them to hold on to their old ways, traditions and loyalties. By not assimilating comprehensively, the immigrants are perceived to be "different" and thus less welcome by existing citizens, further alienating the new immigrants and producing even less integration. The end result is that new immigrants don't completely accept their new country as home, and for the existing citizens it feels less like home because of the changing character of their country. However, even under these conditions, you can be sure that people—new immigrants, old immigrants, natives—would stand, kneel and sit shoulder to shoulder at the church, mosque or temple, listening as one to their religious leaders. Or in many cases, disillusioned by traditional, organized religion, they are drawn to other breakaway sects and variations of religion, sometimes called "New Age spirituality," served by a number of charismatic leaders. Regardless, it will be faith—be it traditional or otherwise—that will bring people together in the future, not the Stars and Stripes or the Union Jack.

Tomorrow's superpowers will not have physical boundaries; their boundaries will be those of the mind and soul. In fact, it will be countries or trade blocs that will divide the faithful of various religions with ever-changing physical borders. And it will be religions—traditional, organized or otherwise—that will unite the far-flung faithful. Those with strong and charismatic leaders will be able to affect and influence the behavior of vast numbers of people, and therefore our world. The mantle of power will fall on religious leaders, be they benevolent and selfless, or power-hungry renegades. It is the likes of Pope Benedict XVI and, yes, even maniacal individuals like [al Qaeda terrorist leader] Osama bin Laden who will have increasing power to influence our world.

As in the past, the conflicts and wars that will rage in our future may not be driven so much by religion per se as by economic factors or scarcity of resources, or simply by people looking for a means to power. However, religion will be the most powerful way to galvanize people to action. We have seen this with Hindus and Muslims in India. Catholics and Protestants in the United Kingdom. Muslims and Jews in the Middle East or Sunnis and Shiites in Iraq. In each case, it is countrymen killing each other in the name of religion. With the continuing march of globalization and its impact on individual identity, it is likely that tomorrow's global leaders will be religious leaders, not political heads of state, and tomorrow's global superpowers will be religions, not nation-states. As such, legitimate leaders of peace-loving religions must recognize this situation as an opportunity to effect positive change in our world and help thwart the efforts of religious fanatics who are using it for their selfish and twisted goals.

Periodical and Internet Sources Bibliography

The following articles have been selected to supplement the diverse views presented in this chapter.

Michelle Gavin	"Africa's Restless Youth," *Current History*, May 2007.
Jason Henderson and Maria Akers	"Coming Home to Rural America: Demographic Shifts in the Tenth District," *Economic Review*, Third Quarter 2009.
Philip Jenkins	"Religion by the Numbers," *Christian Century*, July 13, 2010.
Joel Kotkin	"Ready Set Grow," *Smithsonian*, July/August 2010.
Jon C. Lovett	"Urbanization and Over-population," *African Journal of Ecology*, December 2008.
Ronak B. Patel and Thomas F. Burke	"Urbanization—an Emerging Humanitarian Disaster," *New England Journal of Medicine*, August 20, 2009.
Tim Rieniets	"Shrinking Cities: Causes and Effects of Urban Population Losses in the Twentieth Century," *Nature and Culture*, December 2009.

For Further Discussion

Chapter 1

1. Reread the first two viewpoints in Chapter 1, paying attention to the authors' reasoning concerning the impact of population growth. Do you agree with Michael Fritz's view that the world's increasing population will have devastating effects if it is not limited soon, or do you believe that the *New Internationalist* is correct in arguing that fears about overpopulation are unwarranted? Use quotes from the viewpoints to support your answer.

2. There are situations where ignoring an issue due to political correctness causes a problem to expand to unmanageable levels. In other cases, discussion about and solutions to certain issues can be tainted with discrimination if the debaters are not aware of the impact of the language used and consequences of certain actions. Conduct some outside research, and find articles about population growth. Do you believe that these articles sidestep the issue of population growth, as many people do, according to Tom Flynn, when it comes to this issue for fear of breaking a social taboo? Or, do you think that these articles have racist and elitist undertones, as Andrew Cheeseman contends? Use examples from the articles you find to support your claim.

Chapter 2

1. One of the most oft-cited problems of population growth is environmental decline and resource shortage—a position argued by John and Mary Ellen Harte and David and Marcia Pimentel; however, some experts, such as Fred Pearce, maintain that the consumption level of those al-

ready living on the planet, and not the increasing number of people, is the main threat to the environment and cause of resource depletion. After reading these viewpoints, do you think that overpopulation or overconsumption is a greater threat to the world? Why? Is one problem more easily solved than the other and deserving of greater attention as a result? Explain.

2. While hunger has been declining worldwide for decades, the editors of *Commonweal* worry that continued population growth will lead to food shortages and hunger. Robert Paarlberg disagrees with this notion and states that global food crises will not result from overpopulation but from localized issues such as a lack of rich farmland and susceptibility to global food price increases. Do you think that population growth has the potential to cause more hunger, or do you believe that human technological advances and cooperation among countries are techniques that can be used to contain this problem? Explain your answer, citing the viewpoints.

3. Deborah Rich and Jason Mark outline the ways in which ongoing population growth poses a threat to continued economic growth and stability worldwide. After rereading their viewpoint, decide whether you agree or disagree with their view. Has humanity reached a point at which continued population growth will no longer benefit the global economy as many argue it did in the past? Can sustainable economies be built on growth alone, or must they be restructured so as to function and thrive without continual input from new consumers and workers? Cite the authors to support your claims.

Chapter 3

1. What arguments does Sneha Barot use to support her claim that the United States should support the UN Population Fund? What arguments does Steven W. Mosher ad-

duce in his plea for the United States to discontinue its support of the Population Fund? Whose position do you find more convincing? Explain why.

2. Philip Cafaro and Winthrop Staples III assert that the United States must curb immigration in order to make good on its commitment to sustainability. How do Ian Angus and Simon Butler refute that argument? If you were making US environmental policy, where would you place immigration control on the list of priorities that need to be addressed to ensure a sustainable future? What other concerns, if any, would you place before immigration control? Explain.

Chapter 4

1. Neil Howe and Richard Jackson warn that "youth bulges" in developing countries can herald violence and political instability in those nations. Do you agree that a higher percentage of young people in developing nations is more likely to lead to conflict and extremism? Why or why not?

2. James Kurth believes that declining birthrates will lead nations to become more peaceful because they will not wish to needlessly sacrifice the young to warfare. Reread his viewpoint and decide whether you think his reasoning is sound. What objections might you raise to his optimistic view of humanity's future?

3. What are some of the pros and cons Leiwen Jiang, Malea Hoepf Young, and Karen Hardee see in the ongoing demographic trend toward urbanization? Assuming that this trend continues, do you think urbanization will ultimately have a positive or negative impact on global well-being? Explain your answer, citing from the viewpoints.

Organizations to Contact

The editors have compiled the following list of organizations concerned with the issues debated in this book. The descriptions are derived from materials provided by the organizations. All have publications or information available for interested readers. The list was compiled on the date of publication of the present volume; names; addresses, phone and fax numbers, and e-mail and Internet addresses may change. Be aware that many organizations take several weeks or longer to respond to inquiries, so allow as much time as possible.

Apply the Brakes

e-mail: info@applythebrakes.org
website: www.applythebrakes.org

Apply the Brakes is an online community that grew out of a meeting of conservationists in 2006 that focused on domestic population and consumption growth as the root issues that must be addressed in order to achieve domestic and global sustainability. The website functions as a forum for concerned conservationists to share their ideas about ways in which US population growth can be contained and how its containment will benefit the environment and resource consumption worldwide. Articles on the website include "US Population Past 300 Million, Heading for 400 Million: No Cause for Celebration," "Island Civilization: A Vision for Human Occupancy of Earth in the Fourth Millennium," and "Population Growth and Environmental Sustainability." These commentaries and others can be read on the Apply the Brakes website.

Center for Immigration Studies (CIS)

1522 K Street NW, Suite 820, Washington, DC 20005-1202
(202) 466-8185 • fax: (202) 466-8076
website: www.cis.org

CIS is an organization dedicated to providing information to interested parties concerning the impact of both legal and illegal immigration on the United States. The institute focuses its research on social, economic, environmental, security, and fiscal effects to inform policy makers, the public, and the media about what it sees as the necessary steps that must be taken to address these issues. While the organization's focus is broad, one area of focus is immigration's impact on the environment and population growth. Publications such as "100 Million More: Projecting the Impact of Immigration on the US Population, 2007–2060" and "Immigration to the United States and World-Wide Greenhouse Gas Emissions" can be read on the CIS website.

Institute for Population Studies (IfPopS)

1400 Shattuck Ave., Suite 9, Berkeley, CA   94709
(510) 848-9062
e-mail: info@ifpops.org
website: www.ifpops.org

IfPopS works to encourage people to overcome taboos about discussing overpopulation so that everyone can determine the optimum human population levels for both their region and the globe and then find ways to achieve and stabilize the population at that number. Central to these goals is the work of IfPopS to raise public awareness, which it does by examining the connections between population growth and issues such as sprawl, water rights, and energy consumption, provides funding for population research, and promotes the public discussion of population issues. The organization's website provides extensive information as to why the discussion of population growth is so pertinent in today's world and provides links to numerous other sites addressing this issue. IfPopS runs the website howmany.org, which provides additional information about population growth and information about what individuals can do in response.

Population Connection
2120 L Street NW, Suite 500, Washington, DC   20037
(202) 332-2200 • fax: (202) 332-2302
e-mail: info@populationconnection.org
website: www.populationconnection.org

Population Connection has been active for over four decades in the population control movement. This organization has worked to inform individuals of all ages in the United States about the consequences of continued population growth and to develop family planning policy with the US government that will lead to a sustainable population. The organization focuses on three main areas: protecting the planet, defending women's rights, and ensuring social justice. Extensive information about these topics can be found on the Population Connection website along with previous issues of the organization's magazine, the *Reporter*.

Population Institute (PI)
107 2nd Street NE, Washington, DC   20002
(202) 544-3300 • fax: (202) 544-0068
e-mail: info@populationinstitute.org
website: www.populationinstitute.org

An international nonprofit organization, PI works to ensure that individuals worldwide have equal access to family planning information, education, and services, in order to promote global population levels that allow for a healthy global environment and sufficient resource levels. PI's education programs target policy makers and administrators, the media, and the general public. The institute's publications include reports such as *2030: The "Perfect Storm" Scenario* and *The 2030 Scenario Planning Guide*. The PI website provides access to these reports as well as op-eds, videos, and information about current events.

Population Media Center (PMC)
PO Box 547, Shelburne, VT   05482-0547
(802) 985-8156 • fax: (802) 985-8119

e-mail: pmc@populationmedia.org
website: www.populationmedia.org

PMC employs an entertainment/education approach to promote social change worldwide, focusing on population and reproductive health issues. In particular, the center produces se-
rialized dramas for both radio and television in an effort to
encourage positive behavior change regarding issues such as
environmental preservation, HIV/AIDS, reproductive health
and family planning, women's empowerment, population, and
child protection, modeled after the characters presented in the
programs. Information about the method and theoretical
framework employed by PMC can be found on the
organization's website along with reports about the issues addressed and clips from PMC programs.

Population Research Institute (PRI)

PO Box 1559, Front Royal, VA   22630
(540) 622-5240 • fax: (540) 622-2728
website: www.pop.org

PRI is a nonprofit organization seeking to reveal the truth
about the human rights abuses that often accompany population control programs and show that humans are a great resource to the planet, not a burden on it. The institute created
the site overpopulationisamyth.com with the goal of providing information to debunk what it sees as the overpopulation
myth. PRI also runs a number of programs to fight population control programs and abortion in countries around the
globe. *PRI Review* is the bimonthly publication of the organization; it covers a wide range of issues concerning overpopulation.

Progressives for Immigration Reform (PFIR)

(202) 543-5325 • fax: (202) 543-5332
e-mail: info@pfirdc.org
website: www.progressivesforimmigrationreform.org

Through its educational efforts PFIR seeks to inform the public about the negative, unintended consequences that accompany mass migration, focusing mainly on population size and

growth, workers' wages and conditions, and resource and environmental issues. The organization promotes policies that encourage and aid countries in developing so that the drive to emigrate decreases. In March 2010, PFIR published the report *From Big to Bigger: How Mass Immigration and Population Growth Have Exacerbated America's Ecological Footprint*, describing the ways in which the growing US population threatens the environment. Copies of this report along with additional information about US population growth as a result of immigration can be found on the PFIR website.

Support US Population Stabilization (SUSPS)

PO Box 5654, Berkeley, CA 94705
website: www.susps.org

SUSPS is a coalition of Sierra Club members who are seeking to change the club's official policy regarding immigration and population growth. In light of the Sierra Club's refusal to recognize the SUSPS belief that US population growth, fueled by immigration, is a driving force behind environmental decline, the coalition was formed by concerned members who value ethnic and cultural diversity but want to place a focus on the link between population increases in the United States and environmental degradation. An overview of the issue as well as information about what individuals can do to contribute to the cause can be found on the SUSPS website.

United Nations Population Fund (UNFPA)

605 Third Ave., New York, NY 10158
(212) 297-5000 • fax: (212) 370-0201
e-mail: hq@unfpa.org
website: www.unfpa.org

UNFPA focuses on the interrelated nature of reproductive health, gender inequality, and population and development strategies in an effort to ensure that all people around the world can live healthy lives and have equal opportunities. The organization supports the use of population control programs that assist individuals in making reproductive choices that fit their needs and situations. Publications such as "The State of the World Population 2010: From Conflict and Crisis to Renewal: Generations of Change" can be accessed on the UNFPA website in addition to information about current projects and reports.

World Population Balance
PO Box 23472, Minneapolis, MN   55423
(612) 869-1640
website: www.worldpopulationbalance.org

World Population Balance provides information about current world population levels and educates the public about the ways in which overpopulation is the root cause of problems ranging from resource depletion to species extinction to rising poverty. The organization promotes the notion that a smaller, sustainable population is the first step to addressing these and other issues plaguing the globe today. The World Population Balance website provides details about the world's poorest residents as well as the US population through articles and maps and graphs.

Bibliography of Books

Lester R. Brown, Gary Gardner, and Brian Halweil
Beyond Malthus: Nineteen Dimensions of the Population Challenge. New York: Norton, 1995.

Joel E. Cohen
How Many People Can the Earth Support? New York: Norton, 1995.

Matthew Connelly
Fatal Misconception: The Struggle to Control World Population. Cambridge, MA: Belknap, 2008.

Paul R. Ehrlich
The Population Bomb. Cutchogue, NY: Buccaneer, 1971.

Paul R. Ehrlich and Anne H. Ehrlich
The Population Explosion. New York: Touchstone, 1991.

Ted C. Fishman
Shock of Gray: The Aging of the World's Population and How It Pits Young Against Old, Child Against Parent, Worker Against Boss, Company Against Rival, and Nation Against Nation. New York: Scribner, 2010.

Ronald Freedman, ed.
Population Growth: The Vital Revolution. Piscataway, NJ: Aldine Transaction, 2008.

Betsy Hartmann
Reproductive Rights and Wrongs: The Global Politics of Population Control. Rev. ed. Boston: South End, 1995.

Laurence J. Kotlikoff and Scott Burns — *The Coming Generational Storm: What You Need to Know About America's Economic Future.* Cambridge, MA: MIT Press, 2004.

Massimo Livi-Bacci — *A Concise History of World Population.* 3rd ed. Malden, MA: Blackwell, 2001.

Philip Longman — *The Empty Cradle: How Falling Birthrates Threaten World Prosperity and What to Do About It.* New York: Basic Books, 2004.

George Magnus — *The Age of Aging: How Demographics Are Changing the Global Economy and Our World.* Hoboken, NJ: Wiley, 2008.

Thomas Malthus — *An Essay on the Principle of Population.* Edited by Geoffrey Gilbert. New York: Oxford University Press, 2008.

Jeffrey K. McKee — *Sparing Nature: The Conflict Between Human Population Growth and Earth's Biodiversity.* Piscataway, NJ: Rutgers University Press, 2003.

Donella Meadows, Jorgen Randers, and Dennis Meadows — *Limits to Growth: The 30-Year Update.* White River Junction, VT: Chelsea Green, 2004.

Jane Menken, ed. — *World Population and U.S. Policy: The Choices Ahead.* New York: Norton, 1986.

Steven W. Mosher *Population Control: Real Costs, Illusory Benefits*. Piscataway, NJ: Transaction, 2008.

Fred Pearce *The Coming Population Crash and Our Planet's Surprising Future*. Boston: Beacon, 2010.

Dudley L. Poston Jr. and Leon F. Bouvier *Population and Society: An Introduction to Demography*. New York: Cambridge University Press, 2010.

Maria Ronay *We Have to Change: Taking Action to Stabilize Climate Change, Curb Population Growth Including Immigration, End Poverty, and the Liquidation of Nature's Capital*. Bloomington, IN: iUniverse, 2010.

Frank Trovato, ed. *Population and Society: Essential Readings*. New York: Oxford University Press, 2001.

Mathis Wackernagel and William Rees *Our Ecological Footprint: Reducing Human Impact on the Earth*. Gabriola Island, BC, Canada: New Society, 1998.

Ben J. Wattenberg *Fewer: How the New Demography of Depopulation Will Shape Our Future*. Chicago: Ivan R. Dee, 2004.

John R. Weeks *Population: An Introduction to Concepts and Issues*. Belmont, CA: Wadsworth, 2011.

Index

A

Abortion, reduced recourse to, 119
Acid rain, 53, 55
Adding It Up (Guttmacher Institute report), 116
Africa
    abortion safety, 119
    acid rain problem, 55
    hunger problems, 86
    indigenous farming methods, 80
    informal city settlements, 186
    Kenyatta University, 15
    Population Reference Bureau birth data, 14
    resource consumption, 62
African Executive (magazine), 15
Age structure, importance of, 100–101
Air-Land Battle Doctrine, 178
al Qaeda global terrorist group, 168, 200
Amazon rainforest, 53
American Enterprise Institute, 158
Angus, Ian, 146–155
Anti-immigrant environmentalism, 44
Asia
    air pollution, 190
    echo-booms, 165
    economic achievements, 104, 107
    falling fertility rates, 100–101
    food price fluctuation immunity, 82–84
    hungry people data, 79

    Population Reference Bureau birth data, 14
    poverty reduction efforts, 122
    religious growth, 169–170
    rice-exporting countries, 85
    wheat production, 77
Australia
    conservation/sustainability activism, 154
    resource consumption, 61–62
    Socialist Alliance, 147
    Socialist Alternative (collective), 42

B

Baird, Joni, 112–113
Barajas-Román, Elizabeth, 112–113
Barot, Sneha, 114–125
Battini, Nicoletta, 106
Benedict XVI (Pope), 78, 200
Bernanke, Ben S., 84–85
Bill and Melinda Gates Foundation, 80
Bin Laden, Osama, 200
Biofuels, 71–72
Bloom, David E., 98–109
Borlaug, Norman, 38, 77, 79–80
Bread for the World (organization), 80
Bremmer, Ian, 171
British Medical Journal, 38
British National Party (BNP), 151
Brown, Lester R., 84

declining global numbers, 15,
20, 23, 30–31, 162
economic development and,
122
health provision association,
32
sub-Saharan Africa, 14
total fertility rate (US), 135,
144
young women's education
and, 121
Financial Resource Flows for Population Activities (UN Population
Fund), 124
Flannery, Tim, 149
Flynn, Tom, 35–40
Food shortages, 38
cereal grain changes, 68–69
countries blocking exports, 85
diminishing availability, 67–69
energy supplies, 69–72
lack of modern farming
methods, 87
local vs. global issues, 83–84
roots of shortage panics,
84–85
2008 crisis, 48–49
UN starvation projections, 77
water supplies, 69
See also Hunger
Foreign Affairs article (2010), 158–
159
Fossil fuel consumption, 38
Fossil fuels
acidity contribution, 53–54
carbon tax for usage, 58
human toll of, 72–73
reserve projections, 16
supply limitations, 38
US consumption, 70–71,
74–75
Free Inquiry (journal), 36, 37

Friedman, Thomas, 25
Fritz, Michael, 21–27

G

General Motors, 45
Genetically modified seed, 80
Genocide, 41, 43, 167
Germany
financial resource flows, 124
gross domestic product, 91–92
religious historical background, 198
resource consumption, 61–62
Gittins, Ross, 152–153
Global citizenship, 142–143
Global economic downturn, 62–63
Global gag rule (Mexico City
policy), 115
Global warming, 21, 24
CIA warnings, 26–27
exacerbating factors, 38, 54,
70
as feedback example, 56–57
Gore's acceptance of, 42
Globalization
modern world outcomes, 197
religion and, 200
16th-century spike, 196
Gore, Al, 24, 42, 140
Graham, Otis, 151
Grand Council of the Iroquois,
136
*The Graying of the Great Powers:
Demography and Geopolitics in
the 21st Century* (Howe and
Jackson), 160
Graying (aging) populations
developing-world median age,
162
global impact of, 161–162